parenting

Love in
Spoonfuls

Recipes by **Sarah Putman Clegg**

Photographs by **Erin Kunkel**

CHRONICLE BOOKS

SAN FRANCISCO

contents

ready, set, feed that baby!

Cute coated spoons? Check. Colorful dishes? Yup. Adorable wipe-clean bibs?
Got tons. You've been counting the days and lining up supplies as you approach
this exciting milestone: your baby's first solid food. It's an early step toward
independence for babies and moms, but it is fraught with questions.

How will you know when she's ready to dig in, and what's the best way
to begin? How much should he be eating at 6, 9, or 12 months? How
can you get her to love vegetables, or is it a lost cause? Can you find
time in your jam-packed week to prepare homemade baby food?

The answer to that last question, at least, is yes. (We'll help you answer
the rest, too.) Making homemade food for your baby is easy, fun, and
rewarding—and it can fit into even a busy parent's schedule. That
said, there will inevitably be days when you just want to open a jar,
and that's fine, too; there are plenty of safe, high-quality prepared
baby foods on the market. For those other days, this book will show
you the basics of preparing baby foods at home, helping you find
a balance that works for your family.

Read on for an overview of when and how to introduce solid food to your
baby (and be sure to get your doctor's advice before you start, too); four
chapters of easy, wholesome recipes that grow with your child; and tips for
streamlining kitchen time so you can relax at the table with your family.

family fare

Moms are looking
to put a good meal on
the table for everyone—
not to cook once for the
baby and again for everyone
else. As you move through this
book's chapters, you'll see the
recipes evolving from baby
mush to real table food as soon
as little ones are able to handle
it, with tips for making the
dishes work for grown-ups,
too. Gradually moving baby
toward table food benefits
the whole family!

baby feeding dilemmas solved!

People love to give new moms advice, and you're bound to hear contradictory information when it comes to feeding. The "rules" change over time. Luckily, the current thinking on how and what to start feeding is loosening up, so let your instincts and your baby be your guides.

when should I start?

There's no rush. Until the age of 6 months, babies get all the nutrition they need from breast milk or formula. Some doctors suggest parents wait until 6 months to begin solids; the American Academy of Pediatrics (AAP) says any time between 4 and 6 months is fine. It's up to you—and your baby. Talk to your pediatrician to get her opinion, and watch your baby for the telltale signs she's ready.

what should I start with?

Grandma may insist that you start with rice cereal, but don't feel obliged to go this route. It's fine to offer a fruit, vegetable, or even meat. Whatever you choose, ease into the first meal with some of your baby's usual breast milk or formula. Then offer the "solid" food, which should be pureed smooth and mixed with enough breast milk, formula, or water to thin it.

how will I know my baby is ready?

Your baby sits well on her own and shows good head and neck control; drinks more than 32 fl oz (1 l) of formula a day or, when nursing, pulls off and looks around as if searching for a snack; gazes at you longingly when you eat (and may even try to grab some food for herself!); and can swallow food rather than reflexively pushing it out of her mouth with her tongue.

how much/often should my baby eat?

The answer to this one is simple: just as much as your baby wants, and no more. For the first month or so, offer 1 meal a day of 1 tsp to 1 tbsp puree. By 7 to 8 months, offer as much puree as your baby wants twice a day. At 9 to 11 months, move to 3 meals a day and offer finger foods. By 1 year, your baby may want 3 meals a day and 2 snacks, all table foods.

preparing & storing baby food

For new eaters, all you really need to do is cook each food until it is thoroughly tender and then puree it until smooth in a blender or food processor. In the early days, add liquid to the puree to make it similar in consistency to breast milk or formula; gradually, you'll leave it thicker as your baby becomes accustomed to it.

defrosting puree

Using a microwave is the most convenient method, with precautions:

- Place cube(s) of puree in a microwave-safe bowl and heat on high for 30 seconds to 1 minute to thaw.

- If puree needs more warming, or to reheat refrigerated puree, warm for only 5 to 10 seconds at a time. Stir thoroughly and then taste it yourself to make sure it's not too hot.

freezing baby food

The secret to making baby food at home is to cook big batches and freeze them in serving-sized portions in ice-cube trays. As your baby grows into a toddler, you can continue to freeze a supply of homemade foods. Every recipe in this book tells you whether a food can be frozen, and for how long.

Let purees cool before pouring them into trays and freezing. Once they are frozen solid, transfer the cubes to zippered freezer bags, label, and date. After a few weeks, your freezer will be well stocked with colorful cubes of baby food. As a general rule of thumb, meat purees freeze well for up to 3 months and fruit and vegetable purees freeze well for up to 6 months.

thawing 101

You've likely heard that incorrect thawing can be dangerous, or that a thawed food should not be refrozen. Here's the scoop on what's safe and what's not.

DO thaw foods overnight in the refrigerator, or in the microwave.

DON'T thaw foods by letting them sit at room temperature.

If you thaw frozen fruits and vegetables correctly, you can puree and refreeze them safely. Avoid thawing and refreezing meat or poultry.

first bites

4 to 6 months

feeding a 4- to 6-month-old

Your baby's first meals should be an easy introduction to solid foods. Offer just one food at a time to start. First foods need not be bland but should be easy to digest. Puree the food and thin it to a runny, liquid consistency with breast milk, formula, or water. Let her try each new food for a few days before introducing another.

baby food trends

According to a recent *Babytalk* magazine poll, pureed fruit is the first mush of choice for most parents. Here are current favorite first foods, ranked in order of popularity:

1 Bananas

2 Sweet potatoes

3 Apples

4 Carrots

5 Peas

6 Squash

7 Green beans

8 Pears

how to start

Although fortified rice cereal is traditionally recommended as an ideal first food because it's easy to digest, unlikely to trigger allergies, and a good source of iron, it's safe to offer other foods first. In fact, if your baby has been exclusively breastfed, consider meat; it's a particularly rich source of iron and zinc. A baby's stores of these minerals are depleted by 6 months, and breast milk alone doesn't supply enough of them. Some parents swear by fruit as a first food; it's sweet like breast milk and can be an easy transition. Ask your doctor whether she prefers a specific schedule or pattern.

Pick a time when your little one is in a happy mood—right before the second feeding of the day is a good possibility. Take the edge off her hunger with a short nursing session or a small bottle. Start with a dollop of food on a fingertip; after a few days, increase the meal to a teaspoon and eventually a tablespoon. Don't worry if most of it dribbles down her chin—for the time being, she's getting used to the new flavor and texture.

how to progress

After a few days of the first food with no adverse reaction, such as a rash or vomiting, go on to another food. On the menu are single-grain baby cereals like oatmeal and barley, pureed fruits and veggies, and pureed meats—feed just a spoonful or two once a day.

Give her each new item for 3 days before introducing another food. This way, if your baby has an adverse reaction, you'll know what caused it. New foods can be mixed in with familiar ones. No need to force it; if she's not interested, just try again tomorrow.

what to know about food allergies

The average infant has only a tiny chance of developing food allergies. True food allergies affect only about 5 percent of children. If there is no family history of asthma, hay fever, eczema, or food allergies, this risk is exceedingly small.

But even parents with a family history can relax a bit. Until recently, the advice for them was to delay introducing certain more allergenic foods until the first birthday or beyond. Experts now say that this practice doesn't appear to reduce the incidence of food allergies and that there's no need to delay introducing any allergenic food beyond 6 months. The most allergenic foods, sometimes called the Big Eight, are cow's milk, eggs, nuts, peanuts, wheat, fish, shellfish, and soy.

If one or both parents suffer from allergies, breastfeeding exclusively for the first 6 months and/or using hypoallergenic formula is thought to reduce your baby's risk of developing them. If your child is showing signs of a problem—hives, eczema, vomiting—call the pediatrician. You may need to adjust your child's diet, or your own if you are breastfeeding.

what about water?

When your baby begins solid foods, you can begin to offer a little water in a bottle or cup. But remember that he'll get plenty of water in breast milk or formula as well as from purees. Limit plain water to 4 fl oz (125 ml) a day so that it doesn't displace nutritious foods.

got milk?

Amid the excitement of introducing solids, don't forget that almost all of your baby's nutrition at this age still comes from breast milk or formula—about 32 fl oz (1 l) a day, which means 5 to 8 nursing sessions or 4 to 5 bottles. Solids should complement, not replace, her liquid diet. And save cow's milk until your baby's first birthday. It is hard for infants to digest, and breast milk and formula are tailored to their needs.

red foods

cherries

raspberries

red-skinned apples

red-skinned potatoes

yellow & orange foods

apricots

butternut squash

carrots

peaches

pumpkins

sweet potatoes

golden apples

yellow summer squash

green foods

avocados

green beans

peas

zucchini

blue & purple foods

blackberries

blueberries

serve up the rainbow

At 4 to 6 months, your baby may be eating solid foods only once a day. But as she eats more, and you're wondering what puree to introduce next, think of the rainbow. Offering fruits and vegetables in every color ensures that your little one gets all the nutrients she needs.

what's in a color?

In addition to vitamins and minerals, plant foods contain antioxidants. Often, the very pigment that gives a fruit or vegetable its gorgeous hue is itself a health-promoting antioxidant. Beta-carotene and lycopene, which bring orange and red color to foods, help prevent and repair damage to the body's cells. Blueberries and eggplant contain a beneficial blue compound called anthocyanin, while dark leafy greens offer powerful yellow-hued lutein. And there are thousands more antioxidants. Each benefits different parts of the body—skin, heart, brain, eyes—and the only way to get them all is to eat all the colors of the fresh produce rainbow.

Once your baby is a toddler eating three meals a day, try to offer a variety of colorful fruits and vegetables every day. Think of the rainbow as you feed your family—the more variety of color, the better. It may be easier than you'd think to get your child to eat fruits and vegetables if you focus on color. The choices can be fresh, frozen, canned, dried, or picked up from the supermarket salad bar.

overdosing on orange?

After introducing solids, some parents notice their baby's skin acquiring a faint orangey tinge. So many orange foods are on the "first solids" list—squash, sweet potatoes, carrots—and the beta-carotene in these foods can give one a golden glow, literally. If you notice it, double-check with the doc to make sure it's not jaundice. The cure for carotenemia? Just wait it out: it's not harmful.

the skinny on skins

Sometimes the colorful benefit of a food lies in its skin: think of apples. When your baby is just learning to eat, he'll need tough skins removed, but as soon as he can manage it, start leaving the skins on when you puree his fruits and vegetables. Choose organic for skin-on eating, if you can, to reduce exposure to pesticides.

the dirt on eating green

The scary headlines are hard for any mom to ignore: We're bombarded with reports, studies, and, often, conjecture about whether the way food is grown, harvested, and stored before it gets to our table is harmful or not. The concerns take on new resonance when we have a tiny baby to feed and protect.

The introduction of solid foods is a sensitive period for babies. Pound for pound, babies eat and drink more than adults, so they tend to be exposed to higher concentrations of toxins in food than adults are. As your baby graduates to solid foods and table food, choosing organics at least some of the time can reduce her intake of the pesticides, hormones, and antibiotics commonly used in agriculture today.

the dirty dozen

Thin-skinned fruits and vegetables lead the pack in pesticide load.

1 Peaches
2 Apples
3 Bell peppers
4 Celery
5 Nectarines
6 Strawberries
7 Cherries
8 Leafy greens
9 Grapes (imported)
10 Pears
11 Carrots
12 Potatoes

Eating green is not an all-or-nothing proposition.

what's the bottom line?

That said, don't beat yourself up if you're not going organic with every single food purchase for your family—or even any. Many authorities, including the American Academy of Pediatrics (AAP), don't feel you need to spend the extra dough on these foods. While organic foods are better for the environment, they haven't been proven to be nutritionally superior to conventional food. If you want to go greener, the organic version of certain key foods will have a bigger impact than others. This is good news for families on a budget! For instance, if your baby is mad for peaches, maybe opt to buy organic just for that. The point: Eating green is not an all-or-nothing proposition. Whatever you decide, your baby will thrive.

the scoop on jarred

When you're buying prepared baby food, the same thinking applies: Many experts agree that parents don't really need to spend extra money on organic jarred foods because all baby food manufacturers voluntarily maintain very strict agricultural and cooking practices for even regular baby food. Numerous tests have shown that the levels of pesticide residues in prepared jars are consistently lower than government standards.

Some organic foods have a greater impact than others.

keep it clean

Whether you're preparing conventional produce or organic, there are a few things you can do to make it safer for your baby. Wash produce in warm water and use a vegetable brush to scrub it, then dry with a paper towel. Even bananas and melon can use a rinse. If you like, fill a spray bottle with a blend of 1 part white vinegar to 3 parts water to get your veggies squeaky clean. Washing this way removes more pesticide residue, germs, and wax than washing in cold water alone and air drying.

be strategic

Once your baby is eating a regular solid-food diet, consider buying his favorite, most commonly eaten foods in organic form at least some of the time. Aside from thin-skinned fruits and vegetables, meat and milk are good choices because pesticide residues are stored in fat. Your baby will grow up healthy and strong with a well-balanced, nutritious diet, free of as many *processed* foods as possible, organic or not.

what does "organic" mean?

Before a food can be labeled "organic," it must meet certain standards set by the U.S. Department of Agriculture. It must be grown or produced without the use of chemical pesticides, synthetic fertilizers or sewage sludge, bioengineering, or ionizing radiation. Meat, poultry, eggs, and dairy products must come from animals that are not given antibiotics or growth hormones.

winter squash puree

25 minutes
(mostly hands-off)

freezer safe

makes 1 to 1½ cups
(8 to 12 fl oz/
250 to 375 ml)

Butternut and acorn squash are great starter foods, mild and easy to digest. Orange-fleshed squashes are rich in beta-carotene as well as vitamins A and C, minerals, and fiber. Look for precut squash or choose frozen squash—no need to thaw it before popping it in the oven.

1 tbsp olive oil

one 8-oz (250-g) bag precut fresh or frozen winter squash

water, breast milk, or infant formula, as needed

1 Preheat the oven to 400°F (200°C). Line a rimmed baking sheet with foil.

2 In a large bowl, combine the olive oil and squash. Using your hands, toss the squash to coat lightly with oil. Spread the squash on the prepared baking sheet. Roast the squash until very tender when pierced with a knife, about 20 minutes.

3 Puree the squash in a food processor or blender until smooth. If needed, push through a sieve with a rubber spatula, then add desired liquid to thin the puree to a texture your baby can handle. Check the temperature and serve.

4 To store, refrigerate in an airtight container for up to 3 days, or spoon into ice-cube trays or other freezer containers and freeze, covered, for up to 3 months.

starting whole

Roasting a whole squash is also easy. Halve it and place cut sides down in a baking pan. Add ¼ inch (6 mm) of water and roast at 350°F (180°C) until tender when pierced with a knife, about 1 hour.

toddler variation

You can keep on roasting squash this way long after your baby passes the puree stage. As she grows, you can start adding pepper and dried or minced fresh herbs (try rosemary or sage). Cut the roasted squash into smaller pieces for finger food or use it to make Barley with Butternut Squash (page 130).

root vegetable purees

Root vegetables are packed with nutrients, the root being where a plant stores complex carbohydrates, vitamins, and minerals. Potato and sweet potato are mild and meaty, good choices for your baby's first meals. Once your baby has tried potatoes a few times, blend in turnip or rutabaga for a new flavor.

potato puree

1 hour

freezer safe

makes 1 cup
(8 fl oz/250 ml)

1 russet potato

water, breast milk, or infant formula, as needed

1 Preheat the oven to 425°F (220°C). Pierce the potato 3 or 4 times and bake until tender when pierced with a knife, 1 hour. Let stand until cool enough to handle. Cut the potato in half and scoop out the flesh, discarding the skin.

2 Mash the potato flesh with a potato masher until smooth. If needed, push through a sieve with a rubber spatula, then add desired liquid to thin the puree. Check the temperature and serve. Store in the fridge for up to 3 days or freeze for up to 3 months.

sweet potato puree

25 minutes

freezer safe

makes 2 cups
(16 fl oz/500 ml)

one 16-oz (500-g) bag precut fresh or frozen sweet potato

1 tbsp olive oil

water, breast milk, or infant formula, as needed

1 Preheat the oven to 400°F (200°C). Line a rimmed baking sheet with foil. In a large bowl, combine the sweet potato and oil and toss to coat lightly. Spread the sweet potato on the baking sheet and roast until very tender when pierced with a knife, about 20 minutes.

2 Puree the sweet potato in a food processor or blender just until smooth. If needed, push through a sieve with a rubber spatula, then add desired liquid to thin the puree. Check the temperature and serve. Store in the fridge for up to 3 days or freeze for up to 3 months.

turnip puree

15 minutes

freezer safe

makes 1 cup
(8 fl oz/250 ml)

1 medium or
2 small turnips,
peeled and
chopped

1 tbsp olive oil

water, breast milk,
or infant formula,
as needed

1. In a saucepan over high heat, combine the turnip and oil and add about $^1/_3$ cup (3 fl oz/80 ml) water. Bring to a boil, then cover and reduce the heat so the mixture simmers. Cook until the turnip is tender and the liquid is mostly evaporated, 10 to 20 minutes. Uncover and boil off the remaining liquid.

2. Puree the turnip in a food processor or blender until smooth. If needed, push through a sieve with a rubber spatula, then add desired liquid to thin the puree. Check the temperature and serve. Store in the fridge for up to 3 days or freeze for up to 3 months.

rutabaga puree

25 minutes

freezer safe

makes 2 cups
(16 fl oz/500 ml)

1 rutabaga, peeled
and cut into cubes

cooking liquid,
breast milk, or
infant formula,
as needed

1. Put the rutabaga in a saucepan and add water to cover by 1 in (2.5 cm). Bring to a boil over high heat, then reduce the heat to medium and simmer until tender, about 20 minutes. Drain, reserving some cooking liquid.

2. Puree the rutabaga in a food processor or blender until smooth. If needed, push through a sieve with a rubber spatula, then add desired liquid to thin the puree. Check the temperature and serve. Store in the fridge for up to 3 days or freeze for up to 3 months.

cherry puree

7 to 8 minutes

freezer safe

makes ¾ cup
(6 fl oz/180 ml)

Cherries, like blueberries, are easy for babies to digest. But even when pureed, they still have some texture, so cooking the puree to soften it is a good idea when you are first introducing it. Use a sieve to strain out bits of cherry skin. Serve it uncooked when you think your baby is ready for more texture.

one 16-oz (500-g) bag frozen sweet cherries, thawed in the fridge

1 Puree the cherries in a food processor or blender until smooth.

2 In a saucepan over medium-low heat, warm the puree until hot and starting to steam, about 5 minutes. If needed, strain through a fine-mesh sieve, pushing the puree through with a rubber spatula. Let cool completely before serving.

3 To store, refrigerate in an airtight container for up to 3 days, or spoon into ice-cube trays or other freezer containers and freeze, covered, for up to 6 months.

start fresh

If fresh cherries are in season, by all means use them. If you have a cherry pitter, you can make quick work of pitting a pile of cherries. Measure out 2 cups (8 oz/250 g) pitted cherries and follow the directions above.

toddler variation

For older babies and toddlers, stir the warm or cooled puree into plain yogurt, cottage cheese, or Warm Cereal (page 40) for a breakfast treat.

pear puree

10 to 15 minutes

freezer safe

makes 1 cup
(8 fl oz/250 ml)

It's no wonder babies love pears—they are among the sweetest, juiciest, and mildest fruits. Moms appreciate them because they are high in fiber and can help relieve constipation. Cooking pears (and other fruits) with the skins on retains more nutrients.

2 pears

1 Cut the pears in half. Using a spoon, scoop out the seeds and cores. Pull off the stems. Cut the halves in half again.

2 **To steam:** Bring 1 in (2.5 cm) water to a boil in a pot. Place the pear quarters in a steamer basket and set it in the pot. Cover and steam until tender when pierced with a knife, 7 to 10 minutes, depending on the ripeness of the pear.

To microwave: Place the quarters in a microwave-safe dish with 2 tbsp water. Cover and microwave on high until tender, about 3 minutes. Let stand for 1 minute.

3 Let cool and scrape the flesh from the skins. Puree the pear flesh in a food processor or blender. Check the temperature and serve.

4 To store, refrigerate in an airtight container for up to 3 days, or spoon into ice-cube trays or other freezer containers and freeze, covered, for up to 3 months.

to cook or not to cook?

Ripe pears are a tender fruit and can be pureed raw for an older baby. But if your baby is 4 to 6 months old and just starting solids, steaming them will help ease digestion.

pea-mint puree

5 to 7 minutes

freezer safe

makes 1½ cups
(12 fl oz/375 ml)

Because of their sweet flavor, peas are often offered as a baby's first green vegetable. After your baby has tried peas on their own a few times, you can start adding a little mint (or another tender herb like basil or tarragon) as a new ingredient. Stir the mint into the finished puree.

one 10-oz (315-g) package frozen peas (about 2 cups)

cooking liquid, breast milk, or infant formula, as needed

1 tbsp minced fresh mint or ½ tbsp dried mint

1 **To boil:** Bring a saucepan of water to a boil over high heat. Add the peas and cook until very tender, mashing easily with a fork, 5 to 7 minutes. Drain in a colander, reserving some cooking liquid, and rinse under cold running water to stop the cooking.

To microwave: Place peas in a microwave-safe dish with 2 tbsp water. Cover and microwave on high for 5 minutes, pausing to stir halfway through the cooking time. Let stand for 2 minutes.

2 Puree the peas in a food processor or blender until smooth. If needed, push through a sieve with a rubber spatula, then add desired liquid to thin the puree. Stir in the mint, if using. Check the temperature and serve.

3 To store, refrigerate in an airtight container for up to 3 days, or spoon into ice-cube trays or other freezer containers and freeze, covered, for up to 6 months.

start fresh

In the spring, when just-picked peas in the pod are in the market, use fresh ones in place of frozen. Buy 2 lb (1 kg) peas in the pod for 2 cups (10 oz/315 g) shelled, and cook them as directed above until tender.

apple puree

20 minutes

freezer safe

makes 1½ cups
(12 fl oz/375 ml)

Once your baby has tried apple puree on its own a few times, give her a mealtime vitamin boost by adding squash. Summer squashes, such as pattypan, crookneck, and zucchini, make good starter vegetables—mild and digestible, they offer many vitamins and minerals, especially vitamin A, magnesium, and potassium.

2 apples

1 medium summer squash or zucchini (optional)

1 Bring 1 in (2.5 cm) water to a boil in a pot. Quarter and core the apples, but leave the peels on (to retain more vitamins). Place the apple quarters in a steamer basket and set it in the pot. If using squash, trim and cut it into 1-in (2.5-cm) chunks and add to basket. Cover and steam until tender when pierced with a knife, about 12 minutes.

2 Let cool, reserving the cooking liquid. Scrape the apple flesh from the skins and puree the apple and squash, if using, in a food processor or blender until smooth. Add reserved cooking liquid to thin the puree to a texture your baby can handle. Check the temperature and serve.

3 To store, refrigerate in an airtight container for up to 3 days, or spoon into ice-cube trays or other freezer containers and freeze, covered, for up to 6 months.

family fare

You can use Apple Puree as a sauce for more advanced meals: as a dip for Little Chicken Dippers (page 95) or Salmon Patties (page 98); as a topping for waffles or pancakes; or as an accompaniment to Veggie Pancakes (page 118).

creamy avocado puree

5 minutes

freezer safe

makes about
½ cup
(4 fl oz/125 ml)

You might think of avocados as vegetables, but they are actually a not-very-sweet fruit. What they lack in sweetness they make up for in smooth, creamy, luxurious texture and lip-smacking flavor. Packed with protein, heart-healthy fat, fiber, B vitamins, and zinc, they are a great first food for your baby.

½ **large avocado**

**water, breast milk,
or infant formula,
as needed**

1 Remove the pit from the avocado half and scoop the flesh into a fine-mesh sieve set over a small bowl. Push and scrape the avocado through with a rubber spatula, then scrape it from the bottom of the sieve into the bowl.

2 Stir in ¼ cup (2 fl oz/60 ml) or more desired liquid to thin the puree to a texture your baby can handle.

extra creaminess

Once you introduce yogurt to baby (from 6 months on), it can replace the liquid in this puree—use up to ⅓ cup (3 oz/85 g). Later, you can try cream cheese (see page 38).

storage tip

Refrigerate in an airtight container for up to 1 day or freeze for up to 3 months. The avocado will discolor slightly with storage, but this is not harmful. Stirring will return it to a pale green color. Press plastic wrap directly onto the surface to minimize discoloration.

first turkey

10 minutes

freezer safe

makes ½ cup
(4 fl oz/125 ml)

Newborn babies have a store of iron that lasts them about 6 months. After this, they need to receive iron from food. This is a good age to introduce meat—some pediatricians even recommend it as a first food when pureed on its own. Turkey is mild and digestible, so it's a great place to start.

¼ lb (125 g) ground turkey

sugar-free applesauce or Pear Puree (page 26)

1 In a frying pan over medium heat, combine the turkey with 2 tbsp water. Cook, stirring constantly and breaking up the chunks of meat, until the meat is cooked through and no longer pink, 3 to 5 minutes. Remove from the heat and drain the meat, reserving the cooking liquid.

2 Transfer the turkey to a food processor or blender and puree until it forms a smooth paste, 1 minute. Add the reserved cooking liquid or water, 1 tbsp at a time, to thin the puree to a texture your baby can handle.

3 Stir in the applesauce as needed to make the pureed meat smooth and palatable. Check the temperature and serve.

4 To store, refrigerate in an airtight container for up to 3 days, or spoon into ice-cube trays or other freezer containers and freeze, covered, for up to 3 months.

family fare

You can cook up just a little portion of ground turkey this way for your baby, and use the rest to make turkey burgers for the rest of the family.

time saver

You can puree any well-cooked turkey you have on hand, but ground turkey is quick and easy to prepare. Plus, it's usually made with dark meat, which contains more iron than the white meat.

first lamb

25 minutes

freezer safe

makes ¼ cup
(2 fl oz/60 ml)

Lamb is another good first meat for babies to try—it's lean and easily digestible. It's also rich in iron, which babies 6 months and up need in their diet. For the mildest lamb flavor, try rib chops. These roast quickly in the oven and can become a meal for the whole family. Or, use lamb shoulder steaks and cook them the same way.

**1 lamb rib chop,
1 in (2.5 cm) thick**

1 Preheat the oven to 400°F (200°C). Line a rimmed baking sheet with foil.

2 Place the lamb chop on the prepared baking sheet. Roast until cooked through and no longer pink, turning once, about 10 minutes per side. Remove from the oven and let cool.

3 Trim away the excess fat and cut the meat from the bone. Coarsely chop and puree the meat in a food processor or blender for 1 minute. Add ¼ cup (2 fl oz/60 ml) water and puree until a smooth paste forms. Add more water to thin the puree to a texture your baby can handle. Check the temperature and serve.

4 To store, refrigerate in an airtight container for up to 3 days, or spoon into ice-cube trays or other freezer containers and freeze, covered, for up to 3 months.

fruit combos

If your baby has already tried Prune Puree (page 42) or Dried-Apricot Puree (page 43), try mixing a little into his lamb puree for a smoother texture and sweeter flavor.

flavor explosion

7 to 8 months

feeding a 7- to 8-month-old

By this age, your baby has at least a month of meals under her belt. She's getting better at mashing and swallowing her food, so you can start to challenge her more with new textures. Watch your baby as she eats and you'll soon be an expert on how thick a puree she can handle.

how to start

The introduction of new single-ingredient foods should continue steadily. Not every new food will be a hit at first. It may take 10 to 15 tries (or even more) to get your baby to eat a particular food. You can also start to mix familiar foods together; see the recipes in this chapter for some ideas. Offer solids twice a day. If he's eating a total of 2 to 4 tbsp at each meal and is interested in more, work up to a third meal.

how to progress

Thicker textures are next, so you can add less liquid to purees and try thicker foods like silken tofu. Now that your baby is used to digesting food, she can try the easy-on-the-belly dairy, like whole-milk yogurt and small-curd cottage cheese. How much food does she need now? Let your baby be your guide—some days she'll polish off 1/4 cup (2 fl oz/60 ml) or more; other times, she'll eat half as much. And that's perfectly okay.

what to skip

Try not to overwhelm your baby with too many new foods at once. Remember to introduce new foods one at a time and to serve each for 3 or 4 days in a row before trying the next one. This way you'll know what's bothering your baby if he has a reaction. Treat any seasonings, like herbs and spices, as if they were new foods.

got milk?

Your baby will drink a bit less breast milk or formula now that he's eating more, but it's still his main source of nutrition. He should have 24 to 32 fl oz (750 ml to 1 l) of liquid (4 to 5 bottles or 5 to 8 nursing sessions) daily. As for juice, up to 4 fl oz (125 ml) a day can be offered now, diluted with water if desired, but whole fruits are more nutritious. Juice is high in sugar and excessive amounts can lead to cavities and a less nutritious diet overall. Always check the label to be sure you're buying 100 percent juice, no sugar added.

what about salt?

Hold off, for now. There's no need to add salt to your baby's food just yet. Many foods naturally contain sodium, and too much added sodium can overload her little system and increase risk of dehydration.

what to watch for

Around 8 months, babies develop a fascination with tiny objects (such as morsels of food) and are working on their pincer grasp (holding objects between the thumb and forefinger). When you notice this development, use it to your advantage by offering beginner finger foods. Everything should be cut to the size of your pinkie fingernail and be very soft. Some ideas:

- tiny cubes of banana and avocado
- tiny cubes of tofu
- mashed potatoes
- small slices of soft, ripe fresh fruit or cooked fruit

big kid cups

As soon as your baby can sit up well on her own, she's ready to try a sippy cup. Look for a first cup that's easy to grab and has a soft, nipple-like tip. Some babies need time to accept the novelty of a cup. Let your baby play with the cup as a toy before adding a little liquid and helping him sip. If you introduce juice now, serve it in a sippy cup, not a bottle. Putting breast milk or formula in a cup as well teaches baby that those drinks don't come just from a nipple. When you're ready to start bottle-weaning, try saving the bottle for times when your child most needs comfort (usually just before naptime or bedtime). Keep in mind that the American Association of Pediatrics (AAP) recommends that bottles be gone for good between the first birthday and 18 months.

thicken it up

While the recipes in this chapter still use a food processor or blender for pureeing, you can use other methods as well. A food mill is a great tool for adjusting the thickness of a puree; its interchangeable disks let you determine how thick or smooth you want it. You can also puree one portion of baby's food and just mash the other portion with a fork when you want to go thicker.

introducing dairy

New parents hear it over and over: No cow's milk till your baby turns one. It's good advice. A small percentage of babies are allergic, and for many others, cow's milk protein is just hard to digest. But the rule causes some confusion: Are other dairy products out, too? As it turns out, other dairy can be on the menu earlier.

why it's healthy

Although animal milk is, obviously, designed as food for baby animals, it's also a common food in human cultures all over the world, especially northern Europe. The reason is simple: It's a dense source of nutrition. Milk is loaded with the basic nutrients a growing child needs: fat for brain development; protein for building cells; carbohydrates in the form of lactose, or milk sugar, for energy; calcium for strong bones and teeth; the mineral zinc; and the vitamins A, B_2, B_{12}, and (thanks to fortification) D.

milks people drink

Around the globe you'll find people drinking the milk of these animals:

- buffalo and water buffalo
- camel
- donkey
- goat
- horse
- moose
- reindeer
- sheep
- yak

Dairy is loaded with the basic nutrients a growing child needs.

what to offer

While cow's milk is on hold for babies under one, yogurt is an excellent food to introduce earlier, starting at six or seven months. Why does yogurt get the green light? Yogurt is cultured, meaning healthy bacteria have been added. As these organisms multiply and feed, they break down the milk proteins and make them more digestible. These bacteria live on in our intestines and boost our immune systems. Babies who eat yogurt have more disease-fighting white blood cells and recover more quickly from diarrhea.

cheese

Like yogurt, cheese is also easier to digest than straight milk, in this case because cooking and/or fermenting the milk during the cheesemaking process alters the proteins and makes them more digestible. Make sure any cheese you give your baby is pasteurized; most of the cheese available in the United States is. Good types to start with are soft, fresh cheeses, like cottage cheese and goat cheese.

Start your baby on plain whole-milk yogurt with no added sugars.

allergy & intolerance

Milk allergy is the most common food allergy among young children, but the allergy is rare. Lactose intolerance is also rarer than people think, but more common among people of Asian, Hispanic, or African descent. People who are lactose intolerant lack an enzyme that helps to break down lactose, resulting in bloating and gas. They can often eat cheese and yogurt without trouble.

goat's milk

Goats are much smaller than cows, and the proteins in their milk are smaller and more digestible. Goat's milk also lacks one of the most allergenic proteins found in cow's milk: casein. At six months, breast milk and formula are still the best milks for your baby to drink, but down the road goat's milk can be a better choice for babies who are sensitive to cow's milk. It is lower in folic acid and vitamin B_{12} than cow's milk, so goat milk drinkers need to get these nutrients from other foods.

Q: Do I need to buy "baby yogurt" for my baby?
A: Not necessarily. This is just smart packaging aimed at new moms! Try to start your baby on plain whole-milk yogurt. It's tangier than some yogurts on the market—some of which are so heavily sweetened they are practically puddings. The main thing to look for is that a yogurt contains "live and active cultures" and no added sugar or fillers.

warm cereal

15 minutes

freezer safe

makes ½ cup
(4 fl oz/125 ml)

It's not too early to start teaching your baby to appreciate whole grains. Nowadays brown rice baby cereal and whole-grain oat baby cereal are readily available, but barley can be harder to find in prepared cereal form. Look for pearled barley in the rice aisle or the bulk-food bins.

¼ cup (2 oz/60 g) pearled barley

water, breast milk, or infant formula, as needed

1 In a saucepan over medium-high heat, bring 1 cup (8 fl oz/250 ml) water to a boil. Meanwhile, put the barley in a food processor or blender and grind on high speed until it is reduced to a powder (this will take several minutes).

2 Whisking constantly, slowly pour the powdered grain into the boiling water. Reduce the heat to low and cook, whisking, until the water is absorbed, about 10 minutes.

3 Add desired liquid to thin the cereal to a texture your baby can handle. Check the temperature before serving.

4 To store, refrigerate in an airtight container for up to 3 days, or spoon into ice-cube trays or other freezer containers and freeze, covered, for up to 6 months.

spice it up

You can also combine your baby's cereal with Cherry Puree (page 24) or any other familar fruit puree, or with plain yogurt. Add extra flavor with a pinch of cinnamon or nutmeg, introducing these spices as new foods once your baby is accustomed to the cereal itself.

easy grinding

To grind barley and other grains, your food processor or blender needs to be a powerful one. You can also use a clean coffee grinder. Grind a piece of bread in your coffee grinder to clean out the coffee grounds first.

prune puree

5 to 10 minutes

freezer safe

makes ¼ cup
(2 fl oz/60 ml)

Prunes—or, as the marketers now like to call them, dried plums—are a good source of iron. They are also antioxidant rich and high in vitamins A and C. And, they are famously a natural cure for constipation. Cook prunes to soften them a bit before pureeing. Try mixing this with First Lamb (page 33).

½ cup (3 oz/90 g) pitted prunes

Concord grape juice or water, as needed

1 Coarsely chop the prunes.

2 **To simmer:** In a small saucepan over medium-high heat, combine the prunes with 1½ cups (12 fl oz/375 ml) grape juice (if your baby has tried it already). Bring to a boil, reduce the heat to low, and simmer until tender when pierced with a fork, about 5 minutes. Remove from the heat and let cool, reserving the cooking liquid, until cool enough to handle.

To microwave: Place the prunes in a microwave-safe dish with 2 tbsp grape juice. Cover and microwave on high for 3 minutes. Let stand for 1 minute.

3 Puree the prunes in a food processor or blender until smooth, adding the reserved cooking liquid and/or additional water to thin the puree to a texture your baby can handle. Check the temperature and serve.

4 To store, refrigerate in an airtight container for up to 3 days, or spoon into ice-cube trays or other freezer containers and freeze, covered, for up to 6 months.

dried-apricot puree

5 to 10 minutes

freezer safe

makes ¼ cup
(2 fl oz/60 ml)

Apricots are full of potassium and vitamins A and C—and especially rich in iron in their dried form. Naturally dried fruits are available year-round at farmers' markets, health food stores, and specialty grocers. Swirl this dried-fruit puree into your baby's meats and grains to sweeten them without adding sugar.

½ cup (3 oz/90 g) dried apricots

apple juice or water, as needed

1   Coarsely chop the apricots.

2   **To simmer:** In a small saucepan over medium-high heat, combine the apricots with 1½ cups (12 fl oz/375 ml) apple juice (if your baby has tried it already). Bring to a boil, reduce the heat to low, and simmer until tender when pierced with a fork, about 5 minutes. Remove from the heat and let cool, reserving the cooking liquid, until cool enough to handle.

   To microwave: Place the apricots in a microwave-safe dish with 2 tbsp apple juice. Cover and microwave on high for 3 minutes. Let stand for 1 minute.

3   Puree the apricots in a food processor or blender, adding the reserved cooking liquid and/or additional water to thin the puree to a texture your baby can handle. Check the temperature and serve.

4   To store, refrigerate in an airtight container for up to 3 days, or spoon into ice-cube trays or other freezer containers and freeze, covered, for up to 6 months.

apricot "juice"

If you simmer the apricots, you can serve the remaining cooking liquid to your baby as juice, diluted with water if desired.

raspberry puree

10 minutes

freezer safe

makes 1 to
1½ cups
(8 to 12 fl oz/
250 to 375 ml)

Raspberries are deliciously sweet yet tangy and chock-full of antioxidants to boost your baby's immune system. For sensitive babies, cooking the berries first makes them less allergenic. Blackberries are interchangeable, and trimmed and hulled strawberries may also be used. To skip the strawberry prep, use frozen.

**2 to 3 cups
(8 to 12 oz/250 to
375 g) fresh or
frozen raspberries**

1 Puree the raspberries in a food processor or blender until smooth.

2 If desired, in a saucepan over medium-low heat, warm the puree until hot, about 5 minutes.

3 Strain through a fine-mesh sieve, pushing the puree through with a rubber spatula. If heated, let cool before serving.

4 To store, refrigerate in an airtight container for up to 3 days, or spoon into ice-cube trays or other freezer containers and freeze, covered, for up to 6 months.

family fare

Raspberry Puree can become a perfect sauce for a broiled salmon fillet, sautéed boneless chicken breast, or broiled pork tenderloin. Combine ⅓ cup (3 fl oz/80 ml) each Raspberry Puree and balsamic vinegar with 1 tbsp sugar in a saucepan over medium-high heat. Bring to a boil, then reduce the heat to a simmer until reduced by half and syrupy. Season with salt and pepper to taste and, if you like, toss in a handful of whole raspberries.

cool combinations

Stir this puree into your baby's cereal, or combine it with mashed banana.

fun fruit combinations

Once your baby has tried a variety of individual fruits, you can start to mix and match. Raw peaches, melon, and tropical fruits like mango and kiwi are packed with vitamins and antioxidants, but they can cause allergic reactions in sensitive babies. If you have concerns, simmer the puree for 1 to 2 minutes to mellow it.

banana-mango puree

5 to 10 minutes

freezer safe

makes 1 cup
(8 fl oz/250 ml)

1 mango or 1 cup (6 oz/185 g) frozen mango chunks

1 banana, broken into chunks

water as needed

1 If using a fresh mango, peel, pit, and cut it into chunks. Combine the mango and banana in a food processor or blender. Puree until smooth. If desired, strain through a fine-mesh sieve, pushing the puree through with a rubber spatula.

2 Add water as needed to thin the puree to a texture your baby can handle. Cover and store in the fridge for up to 2 days or freeze for up to 3 months.

blueberry-peach puree

10 minutes

freezer safe

makes 3 cups
(24 fl oz/750 ml)

16 oz (500 g) frozen or fresh peach slices

one 16-oz (500-g) bag frozen or fresh blueberries

water as needed

1 Combine the peaches and blueberries in a food processor or blender and puree until smooth. If desired, strain through a fine-mesh sieve, pushing the puree through with a rubber spatula.

2 Add water as needed to thin the puree to a texture your baby can handle. Cover and store in the fridge for up to 3 days or freeze for up to 6 months.

grape-kiwi puree

5 minutes

freezer safe

makes ¼ cup
(2 fl oz/60 ml)

1 kiwifruit

½ cup (3 oz/90 g) seedless grapes

water as needed

1 Cut the ends from the kiwifruit, then use a vegetable peeler or paring knife to remove the fuzzy skin. Cut into chunks.

2 Combine the kiwifruit and grapes in a food processor or blender and puree until smooth. To remove the grape skins, strain through a fine-mesh sieve, pushing the puree through with a rubber spatula.

3 Add water as needed to thin the puree to a texture your baby can handle. Cover and store in the fridge for up to 3 days or freeze for up to 3 months.

banana-cantaloupe puree

5 minutes

freezer safe

makes 1 cup
(8 fl oz/250 ml)

¼ cantaloupe or 1 cup (6 oz/185 g) precut cantaloupe chunks

1 banana, broken into chunks

water as needed

1 Cut the cantaloupe quarter into slices, then peel the slices. Cut the flesh into chunks.

2 Combine the cantaloupe and banana in a food processor or blender and puree until smooth. If desired, strain through a fine-mesh sieve, pushing the puree through with a rubber spatula.

3 Add water as needed to thin the puree to a texture your baby can handle. Cover and store in the fridge for up to 2 days or freeze for up to 3 months.

asparagus & applesauce puree

10 to 12 minutes

freezer safe

makes 1 cup
(8 fl oz/250 ml)

The wider the range of foods a baby tries during the first year, the more likely he is to return to eating a wide range of foods later on. Once they turn 1 or 1½, many babies enter a picky phase. So by all means, try out asparagus on your little guinea pig! He may surprise you and gobble it up…for now.

12 oz (375 g) fresh or frozen asparagus

⅓ cup (3 fl oz/ 80 ml) sugar-free applesauce

1 If using fresh asparagus, cut off the woody bottoms of the stalks and cut the tender portions into 1-in (2.5-cm) lengths.

2 **To steam:** Fill a large pot with 1 in (2.5 cm) water and bring to a boil over medium-high heat. Put the asparagus in a steamer basket, set in the pot, cover, and steam until tender, about 7 minutes for frozen or 9 minutes for fresh. Rinse under cold running water to stop the cooking.

To microwave: Place the asparagus in a microwave-safe dish with 2 tbsp water. Cover and microwave on high until tender, about 5 minutes for frozen or 7 minutes for fresh. Let stand for 1 minute.

3 Puree the asparagus in a food processor or blender until smooth. Stir in a little applesauce to smooth and sweeten the puree. Check the temperature and serve.

4 To store, refrigerate in an airtight container for up to 3 days, or spoon into ice-cube trays or other freezer containers and freeze, covered, for up to 3 months.

slender spears

When shopping for asparagus for your baby, choose young, slender spears if possible. These are less fibrous than thicker spears and need no peeling. Asparagus is high in vitamin C, vitamin K, and especially folate (vitamin B9, which helps prevent birth defects), making it an ideal food for the early stages of pregnancy.

pumpkin soup

25 minutes
(mostly hands-off)

freezer safe

makes 4 cups
(32 fl oz/1 l)

Get your baby accustomed to eating soup now; when he's a toddler, you'll find it's a great way to sneak all sorts of unpopular veggies into his diet. If you don't have leftover cooked rice handy, use instant. Canned pumpkin is concentrated and contains less water than fresh, so it contains more vitamins ounce for ounce.

one 15-oz (470-g) can pumpkin puree

1 cup (5 oz/155 g) cooked white or brown rice

¼ tsp pepper

1 In a saucepan over medium-high heat, combine the pumpkin, 4 cups (32 fl oz/1 l) water, rice, and pepper. Bring to a boil, cover, and reduce the heat to medium-low. Simmer until the rice is very soft, about 20 minutes.

2 Let cool slightly, then puree in batches in a food processor or blender until smooth. Check the temperature before serving.

3 To store, refrigerate in an airtight container for up to 3 days, or spoon into ice-cube trays or other freezer containers and freeze, covered, for up to 6 months.

the scoop on broth

As your baby gets older, anytime after 6 months, try replacing the water in this soup with chicken broth for more flavor. When buying chicken broth for your baby's food, look for a low-sodium broth with as few ingredients as possible and make sure your baby has tried them all separately. You can always add salt to taste but you can't take it out.

spice it up

Stir a spoonful of plain yogurt into the soup just before serving, and sprinkle with cinnamon once your baby has tried each of these foods on its own. As your child starts eating more dairy, you can replace the yogurt with a little cream.

carrot-apple medley

20 minutes
(mostly hands-off)

freezer safe

makes 2 cups
(16 fl oz/500 ml)

Once your baby is accustomed to this dish, you can add a spice or herb to liven it up and introduce a new flavor. Try a grinding of pepper; a pinch of ginger, cinnamon, or cumin; or a sprinkle of chopped fresh or dried parsley, mint, or cilantro. Introduce a spice or herb as you would any other new food.

1 lb (500 g) baby-cut or other peeled carrots

2 tbsp olive oil

1 cup (8 fl oz/ 250 ml) sugar-free applesauce

water, breast milk, or infant formula, as needed

1 In a saucepan over high heat, combine the carrots, 1/2 cup (4 fl oz/ 125 ml) water, and the olive oil. Bring to a boil, then lower the heat to medium-low, cover, and simmer until the carrots are nearly tender, about 12 minutes.

2 Uncover, raise the heat to medium, and continue cooking, stirring occasionally, until the water has evaporated and the carrots are tender and glistening, 3 to 4 minutes longer.

3 Puree the carrots and applesauce in a food processor or blender; it may take up to 2 minutes before it is completely smooth. Add desired liquid to thin the puree to a texture your baby can handle. Check the temperature and serve.

4 To store, refrigerate in an airtight container for up to 3 days, or spoon into ice-cube trays or other freezer containers and freeze, covered, for up to 6 months.

variation

For toddlers, add some pepper before cooking the carrots. Skip the pureeing with applesauce in Step 3, and serve the glazed carrots chopped or sliced on the diagonal and topped with a sprinkling of an herb or spice.

first chicken

15 to 25 minutes

freezer safe

makes 1½ to 1¾ cups
(12 to 14 fl oz/
375 to 430 ml)

Here are two basic methods of cooking chicken that can be used to create a variety of textures and meals for your baby. Baking in the oven works especially well for flavorful, fattier, and iron-rich thighs, while poaching keeps lean meat moist and juicy, making it an ideal method for chicken breasts.

½ to ¾ lb (250 to 375 g) boneless, skinless thighs or chicken breast

olive oil spray (if needed for baking)

fruit or vegetable puree or Warm Cereal (page 40), as needed (optional)

1 **To bake chicken thighs:** Preheat the oven to 400°F (200°C). Line a baking sheet with foil. Lightly spray the chicken thighs with oil and place on the prepared sheet. Bake, turning once, until the chicken is cooked through and no longer pink in the center, about 20 minutes.

To poach chicken breasts: If the chicken breast is thicker than 1 in (2.5 cm), slice it horizontally almost all the way across, then open the 2 halves like a book. In a frying pan over medium-high heat, bring about ¼ in (6 mm) water to a simmer. Add the chicken; the water should come about halfway up the sides of the chicken. Adjust the heat to keep the water barely simmering. Cook, turning once, until cooked through and no longer pink in the center, 8 to 12 minutes. Transfer to a cutting board and reserve the cooking liquid.

2 Chop the cooked chicken coarsely, transfer to a food processor or blender, and puree for 1 minute. The texture will be clumpy. Add the reserved cooking liquid or water 1 tbsp at a time as needed to make a smooth paste. Add puree or cereal as desired to make the pureed meat smooth and palatable. Check the temperature and serve.

3 To store, refrigerate in an airtight container for up to 3 days, or spoon into ice-cube trays or other freezer containers and freeze, covered, for up to 3 months.

family fare

Small chicken bites (the size of your pinkie nail) or needle-like strips make great finger foods for toddlers to dip in Hummus (page 78) or Banana & Avocado Guacamole (page 82). Chicken breasts can be used in salads and pastas for adults.

your baby's palate

Just as every imaginable hue can be described as a combination of the three primary colors, the flavors we enjoy can be described as a combination of five basic tastes. Our tongues and the lining of our mouths are dotted with taste bud receptors, each designed to perceive one of the five kinds of tastes:

Sweet Sweetness is a sign that a food contains sugar, for a boost of calories and energy. Babies learn early on to seek out this flavor: breast milk is sweet. These taste receptors are clustered in the front of the tongue, so just one little lick lets a baby know he's on to something sweet.

Salty Saltiness is another taste preferred by babies in their primitive quest for nutrients. This taste signals sodium, a nutrient essential to the heart and nervous system. Like sweet taste buds, the salty ones are clustered around the front tip of the tongue.

Bitter Bitter flavors are sensed most strongly at the back of the tongue. Children have an aversion to bitter flavors, which may even trigger a gag reflex. There's a good reason for this: Many toxic plants taste bitter, so bitterness is a natural red flag.

Sour Sour receptors are located on the sides of the tongue. Sour flavors are less popular among babies than sweet and salty—another possible protective instinct that helps them avoid spoiled food—but older children often relish sourness in fruits.

Umami This savory fifth flavor (whose name means "yummy" in Japanese) was officially recognized outside of Asia in 2002, when the taste receptor for it was isolated and cloned. Foods with this subtle quality include mushrooms, meat, dairy, and fish, as well as fermented and aged foods such as cheese, fish sauce, and soy sauce.

tricking the taste buds

Pediatrician Dr. William Sears tells parents to use the arrangement of taste buds on the tongue to help babies accept new flavors. Since babies prefer sweet and salty foods, you can place these foods on the tip of your baby's tongue to give her the full effect. If your baby is wary of new tastes, place new foods toward the middle of the tongue where there are fewer taste receptors, so the flavors will be less intense.

sweet foods

blackberries

cherries

strawberries

salty foods

crackers

olives

pickles

pretzels

bitter foods

bitter leafy greens

broccoli

unsweetened chocolate

umami foods

cheese

meat

mushrooms

soybeans

sour foods

grapes

lemons

oranges

✱ While some of these are not first foods, they represent the five different tastes a baby experiences.

broccoli & goat cheese puree

20 minutes
(mostly hands-off)

freezer safe

makes 1½ cups
(12 fl oz/375 ml)

Microwaving or steaming broccoli is the fastest method of cooking it, but roasting brings out its sweet, delicious flavor—meaning a better chance of turning on your kid to this highly nutritious vegetable. Look for precut florets to save prep time. Add the goat cheese once she's had the broccoli on its own.

one 12-oz (375-g) package precut broccoli florets (about 3 cups)

1 tbsp olive oil

half a 4½-oz (150-g) log fresh goat cheese (pasteurized), broken into chunks

water, breast milk, or infant formula, as needed

1 Preheat the oven to 375°F (190°C). Line a rimmed baking sheet with aluminum foil.

2 Using kitchen shears, snip the broccoli florets into smaller, equal-size pieces. Put the olive oil in the bottom of a large bowl, add the broccoli, and toss to coat. Spread the broccoli on the prepared baking sheet without crowding the pieces. Roast the broccoli until tender and browned, about 15 minutes.

3 Combine the broccoli and ¼ cup (2 fl oz/ 60 ml) water in a food processor or blender. Puree until smooth and add the goat cheese. Puree again to combine into a paste. Add desired liquid to thin the puree to a texture your baby can handle. Check the temperature and serve.

4 To store, refrigerate in an airtight container for up to 3 days, or spoon into ice-cube trays or other freezer containers and freeze, covered, for up to 6 months.

variation

Feel free to substitute cauliflower for the broccoli. It is similarly healthy but milder in flavor. Note that both broccoli and cauliflower can produce gas, so if your baby already tends to be gassy, hold off on introducing these vegetables for a month or two.

spice it up

Researchers have found that even very young babies appreciate the taste of garlic in their mothers' breast milk, so don't be shy about introducing it. You can add a couple of pinches of powdered garlic (not garlic salt!) to this puree to add exciting flavor.

potato-leek soup

30 minutes

freezer safe

makes 2½ cups
(20 fl oz/625 ml)

Leeks add savory flavor and also many of the nutritional benefits of other green vegetables, without the bitter flavor that many babies dislike. As your baby grows older, you can add more layers of flavor to this soup by replacing the water with low-sodium stock and finishing it with a splash of cream.

2 leeks, white parts only

2 russet or sweet potatoes

1 tsp olive oil

water, breast milk, or infant formula, as needed

1 Thinly slice the leeks crosswise. Place in a colander, rinse well to remove any grit, and pat dry. Peel the potatoes and thinly slice them crosswise.

2 In a saucepan over medium-high heat, warm the olive oil. Add the leeks and cook, stirring constantly, until soft, about 3 minutes. Add the potatoes and stir well.

3 Add just enough water to cover the vegetables, about 1 cup (8 fl oz/ 250 ml). Bring to a boil, then reduce the heat to medium-low, cover, and simmer until the vegetables are tender, about 15 minutes.

4 Set a colander over a bowl and drain the vegetables, reserving the cooking liquid. Puree the vegetables in a food processor and add enough of the reserved cooking liquid and desired liquid to thin the soup to a texture your baby can handle. Let cool and serve.

5 To store, refrigerate in an airtight container for up to 3 days, or spoon into ice-cube trays or other freezer containers and freeze, covered, for up to 6 months.

spice it up

Tender herbs such as parsley, basil, tarragon, dill, or a blend are perfect for this soup. Along with the water, add ³/₄ tsp dried herbs or 1½ tsp chopped fresh herbs, introducing each of them as you would any new food.

zucchini–white bean puree

10 minutes

freezer safe

makes 1 cup
(8 fl oz/250 ml)

When choosing canned beans for baby food, look for a low-sodium choice. Some brands use seaweed instead of salt to preserve the beans. Since your baby will eat the zucchini skin, this is a good recipe for going organic. As your baby gets older, try adding minced parsley and 1 or 2 garlic cloves to this puree.

2 large or 3 small zucchini or other summer squash

olive oil, as needed

one 15-oz (470-g) can white beans, rinsed and drained

1 Preheat the broiler and line a baking sheet with foil. Cut the zucchini in half lengthwise, brush the cut sides with olive oil, and slide under the broiler 4 in (10 cm) from the heat source. Cook until tender and golden, 5 to 7 minutes. Let cool slightly, then chop into chunks.

2 Combine the squash and beans in a food processor or blender and puree until fairly smooth (this puree will have some texture). Check the temperature and serve.

3 To store, refrigerate in an airtight container for up to 3 days, or spoon into ice-cube trays or other freezer containers and freeze, covered, for up to 6 months.

scrambled egg

There are differing schools of thought about the correct texture for scrambled eggs. Some say they should be creamy with small curds, while others like them fluffier with big, soft curds. Where you come down probably depends on how your folks made them. Instructions for both styles are given here.

1 large egg

1 tbsp cream, milk, or water

pepper

1 tsp butter

stir-ins (optional; see ideas at right)

1 In a bowl, combine the egg, desired liquid, and a sprinkle of pepper. Beat lightly with a fork just until the egg yolk and white are combined.

2 In a small frying pan over high heat, melt the butter. When it foams, swirl the pan to coat and pour in the egg.

3 **For a fluffy egg:** Keep the heat on high. Use a heatproof rubber spatula to slowly push and fold the eggs in the pan. Cook until the egg is clumped in a single mound but still shiny, 30 to 45 seconds.

For a creamy egg: Reduce the heat to low. Stir constantly with a fork, cooking for 5 to 10 minutes.

4 Just before the egg is done to your liking, transfer to a plate. The egg will continue cooking a bit off the heat. Let cool slightly and serve, cutting up larger curds as needed so baby can manage them.

safety first

Undercooked eggs can carry salmonella. When cooking for a young child, make sure any visible whites are opaque and cooked through. Grown-ups may like their scrambled eggs more lightly cooked, but for safety's sake, always cook children's eggs well.

stir it in

- **cheese** spoon or crumble 1 tbsp ricotta, cottage cheese, goat cheese, or feta onto the egg as it starts to cook

- **veggies** sauté finely diced mushrooms, red pepper, and/or onion in butter for 5 minutes before adding the egg

- **lox** sauté 1 finely chopped slice of lox in butter for 2 minutes before adding the egg

eating adventures

9 to 11 months

feeding a 9- to 11-month-old

Mealtime with your older baby is becoming a freewheeling affair. Your youngster is growing more independent by the day, learning to crawl and stand. She is trying her hand at wielding a spoon, testing the laws of physics by dropping food onto the floor, and testing your patience as she smears it in her hair.

got milk?

At this age, daily breast-milk or formula feedings will diminish to about 3 to 4 bottles or 4 to 6 nursing sessions, totaling 16 to 24 fl oz (500 to 750 ml) of liquid. It may be hard to believe, but until age 1, most of your baby's nutrition still comes from his breast milk or formula; food continues to be mostly about experimentation and experiencing new flavors. Now that your baby has a good repertoire of regular foods, keep pushing the envelope with new flavors and textures.

how to start

If your baby has not tried finger foods already, she'll likely be ready to start now. At every meal, offer a variety of tiny pieces of "real" food. Some favorites are O-shaped cereals, small cooked pasta pieces, shredded chicken or flaked fish, well-cooked peas, finely diced well-cooked carrots, and scrambled eggs. By 9 months, babies can generally gnaw hard bready foods like teething biscuits and bagels, as long as parents keep a close watch. (See page 92 for more finger-food ideas.) Here are the sure signs that your baby can play a more active role at mealtime:

- Your baby has choppers. Even babies who are slow to teethe can gum soft finger foods very well, but teeth are a natural sign of readiness for regular foods.

- Your baby can deliberately get food into his own mouth.

- Your baby is constantly trying to put nonfood items in his mouth.

how to progress

By the end of the first year, aim to serve as much "table food" as you can, weaning your baby off mushes and purees. The recipes in this chapter look more like regular food and can be enjoyed by parents as well as your baby. Three meals a day is the goal. Keep introducing new foods one at a time, waiting a few days before trying the next one.

what to watch for

Your tot's more mobile these days—scooting, crawling, reaching, pulling up. Resist letting her nosh while she's on the move, since she could choke if she's trying to toddle and eat at the same time. The safest spot for meals is the high chair, with supervision.

your anti-choking guide

Never serve any of the following foods (or anything like them) to your baby or young toddler:

- whole nuts
- gobs of peanut butter (spread it thinly on a cracker instead)
- popcorn
- raisins or dried-fruit pieces
- sunflower or pumpkin seeds
- hard vegetables or fruits such as raw carrots, raw celery, raw green beans, or raw apples

- hot dogs (only serve them quartered lengthwise and cut into sticks)
- cherry tomatoes or whole grapes (only serve them cut into quarters or smaller)
- hard, gooey, or sticky candy like marshmallows or jellybeans
- chewing gum

If you haven't already, consider taking a first-aid class from the Red Cross to learn the Heimlich maneuver as well as CPR for babies.

what to skip

Cow's milk and honey are still off limits for the first year: Milk proteins aren't easily digested before age 1, and honey may contain the bacteria that cause botulism in babies. By the time they reach age 1, babies' bodies are stronger and mature enough to fight off these bacteria.

whatta mess!

At this age, your baby's really enjoying her meals—especially the part where she squishes and flings her food. There are two tactics you can use to minimize the mess. One is to keep her portions small; scatter only a few pieces of finger food on her tray at a time. Tactic two is to practice your blank face. If you laugh at her antics or scold her you'll only reinforce the behavior.

fish in your baby's dish

Fish has been in the news a lot in recent years: *It's brain food. It's tainted with mercury. It's heart healthy. It's an allergy risk. We should eat it at least once a week.* These conflicting messages can be hard for a new parent to navigate. Here's a quick overview of the current thinking on babies and fish.

yes, fish is brain food

Study after study shows that the omega-3 fatty acids found in fish are essential nutrients for babies' brains. Babies whose mothers take omega-3 supplements during pregnancy and nursing continue to show more powers of concentration and higher cognitive abilities even at the age of four. Omega-3s also help sharpen vision, boost the immune system, and prevent eczema—and can even keep your baby cheerful by boosting his dopamine and serotonin levels! Since the brain develops most rapidly during the first year of life, there is no better time to start getting fish into your baby's diet.

mercury meter

Low mercury: anchovies, catfish, flounder, perch (ocean), salmon*, shad, sole, trout (freshwater), and whitefish

Moderate mercury: carp, cod, halibut*, mahi mahi, monkfish, trout (sea), and tuna (chunk light)*

High mercury: Chilean sea bass, king mackerel, marlin, orange roughy, shark, swordfish, tilefish, and tuna (albacore, yellowfin, bigeye, ahi)

*best sources of omega-3s

Fish might seem like a "grown-up" food, but it is the ideal fare for infants.

you can limit mercury exposure

Some fish are higher in mercury and other pollutants than others. Consult the Mercury Meter at left to find the best choices. (Fish high in mercury also should not be eaten by expectant mothers.) It's fine to consume up to 12 oz of low-mercury fish per week. All in all, salmon is the fish of choice for babies: It's high in omega-3s, but low in mercury. And, it's versatile and family-friendly, making it a hit for busy moms.

Farm-raised salmon is higher in pollutants and may be lower in the healthiest omega-3s than wild, so go for the wild kind when you can (and stick to 6 oz or less per week of the farmed kind). Fresh wild salmon is pricier, but most canned salmon is made with wild varieties, making it a less expensive choice. See page 98 for a delicious recipe for Salmon Patties using canned salmon.

yes, fish is a "big eight" food

True, fish is one of the more common causes of food allergies. But only 5 percent of children have a true food allergy, and experts no longer advise delaying the introduction of certain foods to prevent allergies. This means that you can offer fish to your baby as soon as she's ready for solid foods—from 6 months on is fine. Just be sure to offer it as the only new food for a few days in a row to make sure there's no adverse reaction. If your baby has already shown allergic tendencies, such as an allergic rash, ask your pediatrician about the best time to introduce fish.

what about supplements?

If yours is a fish-phobic family, talk to your child's doctor about supplements. Many baby formulas are now enhanced with DHA, the healthiest kind of omega-3. If you want to offer Junior fish oil, be sure to choose a brand that is highly refined and free of mercury or other contaminants, such as Dr. Sears' GO FISH Children's Omega-3 DHA Liquid or Nordic Naturals. DHA supplements from non-fish sources (like seaweed) are also available.

Offer fish to your baby early on, and it may just become a favorite food.

quick fish tip

Besides canned salmon, frozen fish sticks and salmon burgers are another fast mealtime solution for busy moms of toddlers. Just check the label to make sure they are made from whole fillets without fillers. Whichever fish you're serving, cut it into small pieces or flakes before sharing with your baby. Let your toddler dip in ketchup, tartar sauce, or ranch dressing.

first fish

5 minutes

makes 1 fillet

Fish cooks quickly, and it's easy to overcook. But steaming it in a microwave is surprisingly easy and successful—as long as you keep the fish moist, you'll have delicious fish for your baby's dish in just a few minutes. If you want fish for the whole family, cook one piece at a time for best results.

one 1/3-lb (155-g) fish fillet such as cod, halibut, or salmon

2 tbsp orange juice or water

1 Cut the fillet lengthwise into 2 equal strips, each about 1 in (2.5 cm) wide. If your piece of fish is thicker than 1 in (2.5 cm), butterfly it by cutting horizontally down the length of each strip almost all the way through, then lay the fish flat by opening it like a book.

2 Set the fish in a microwave-safe dish with a lid. Drizzle with the orange juice and cover with the lid. (Use orange juice after your baby has had fish alone.)

3 Place the fish in a microwave oven and cook on high heat until the fish is slightly translucent but still moist in the thickest part (cut into the fish to check), 2 to 3 minutes. Remove the fish from the microwave and let rest for 2 minutes to finish cooking.

4 Use a fork to flake the fish into small pieces. Let cool and serve.

fish and citrus

If your family is allergy prone, be sure to introduce fish and citrus one at a time. Both can cause reactions, such as a rash or upset stomach. Offer each alone for a few days before trying any other new foods.

first pork

When you first introduce pork (or other meat), your baby may appreciate having a little applesauce or pureed pear stirred in to smooth the texture a bit. Pureed meat on its own is a little pasty! As she grows older, try serving this pork stirred into rice, with chopped cooked green beans and a drizzle of olive or sesame oil.

¼ lb (125 g) ground pork

2 pinches ground ginger

fruit or vegetable puree, such as sugar-free applesauce or Pear Puree (page 26)

1 In a small frying pan over medium heat, combine the pork and ginger. Cook, stirring occasionally to break up the meat, until well browned, 7 to 8 minutes. As the meat begins to sizzle, stir more often.

2 For pureed pork, transfer to a food processor or blender and puree for 1 minute; the texture will be crumbly. Add water 1 tbsp at a time as needed to thin the puree to a consistency your baby can handle. Add applesauce as needed to make the pureed meat smooth and palatable. Alternatively, as your baby becomes more adept at chewing, serve the ground pork without pureeing. Check the temperature before serving.

3 To store, refrigerate in an airtight container for up to 3 days, or spoon into ice-cube trays or other freezer containers and freeze, covered, for up to 3 months.

start fresh

Fresh ginger adds extra savory flavor to this dish. Peel a hunk using the edge of a soup spoon (it's easier than using a vegetable peeler). Finely dice or whirl in a food processor to grate. Add 1 tsp in place of the dried ginger; freeze the rest for up to 6 months. Thinly sliced green onions are another savory add-in.

family fare

Older toddlers—and grownups, too—may enjoy eating seasoned ground pork in lettuce cups or wrappers. Use iceberg, butter, or another round-headed lettuce, and separate the leaves to get down to the small cuplike inner ones. Older kids will enjoy scooping the cooked pork into the leaves and rolling them up to make wraps.

first beef

Beef is a good source of protein, B vitamins, and iron for babies. To keep it digestible for tiny stomachs, select a lean cut such as top sirloin steak. Choose organic beef if you can, or grass-fed if available—this type is higher in healthful omega-3 fats than corn-fed beef.

one ¹/₄-lb (125-g) small top sirloin steak, ³/₄ to 1 inch (2 to 2.5 cm) thick

pepper

¹/₄ tsp minced fresh rosemary

vegetable oil spray

fruit or vegetable puree, such as sugar-free applesauce or Sweet Potato Puree (page 22)

1   Sprinkle the steak lightly with pepper and the minced rosemary. Let stand for 15 to 30 minutes to warm to room temperature.

2   Preheat the broiler and line a rimmed baking sheet with foil. Place the steak on the baking sheet and slip under the broiler, about 4 in (10 cm) from the heat source.

3   Broil the steak on the first side for 4 minutes, then turn and cook on the other side for 4 minutes more. Remove the steak from the broiler and cut into it to check that it is well done, especially if your steak is larger than ¹/₄ lb (125 g). Transfer the steak to a cutting board and let stand for a few minutes.

4   For pureed beef, coarsely chop the steak. Transfer to a food processor or blender and puree for 1 minute; the texture will be crumbly. Add water 1 tbsp at a time as needed to thin the puree to a consistency your baby can handle. Add applesauce as needed to make the pureed meat smooth and palatable. Alternatively, as your baby becomes more adept at chewing, serve the ground beef without pureeing. Cut or shred it into tiny pieces. Check the temperature before serving.

5   To store, refrigerate in an airtight container for up to 3 days, or spoon into ice-cube trays or other freezer containers and freeze, covered, for up to 3 months.

creamy pear with spinach

10 minutes

makes 1 cup
(8 fl oz/250 ml)

Once your baby has eaten two of the three main ingredients here—say, pears and yogurt—you can start adding some spinach to the mix for powerful nutrition. Each time you make it, add more spinach to the blend to gradually accustom your baby to the taste.

1 handful fresh spinach leaves

2 tbsp plain yogurt or heavy cream

2 ripe pears, about 1 lb (500 g), peeled, cored, and quartered

1/8 tsp ground nutmeg (optional)

1 Bring a pot of water to a boil over high heat. Add the spinach and cook until wilted, about 1 minute. Drain well. Place the spinach on a clean kitchen towel or paper towels and squeeze until barely moist.

2 Puree the spinach, yogurt or cream, and pear quarters in a food processor or blender until smooth. Stir in the nutmeg, if using, and serve.

3 To store, refrigerate in an airtight container for up to 3 days, or spoon into ice-cube trays or other freezer containers and freeze, covered, for up to 3 months. The pears will discolor slightly, but this is not harmful.

dreamy cream

According to the research of Canadian allergist Janice Joneja, cream is far less allergenic than milk—about on par with oatmeal and avocado, two common first foods. You can offer your baby cream anytime after 6 months, introducing it like any new food.

basic oatmeal

20 minutes

makes about
1½ cups
(12 fl oz/375 ml)

This warm whole-grain cereal, especially when mixed with a little cream, will give your little one stamina for the busy day of crawling, cruising, or toddling ahead. Old-fashioned oats cook up with a good texture. You can make a big batch at the beginning of the week to serve each day with different stir-ins for variety.

1 cup (3 oz/90 g) old-fashioned rolled oats

½ tsp ground cinnamon (optional)

1 tsp vanilla extract (optional)

stir-ins (optional, see ideas at right)

1 In a saucepan over high heat, bring 1½ cups (12 fl oz/375 ml) water to a boil. Stir in the oats and cinnamon and vanilla, if using. When the mixture begins to simmer, cover and remove from the heat. Let stand until tender, about 15 minutes.

2 Stir in flavorings, if desired. Check the temperature and serve.

stir it in

Here are some flavor, color, and texture variations for a single ½-cup (4–fl oz/125-ml) portion:

- ¼ banana, mashed, plus 1 tbsp Raspberry Puree (page 45)
- 2 tbsp canned pumpkin puree
- 2 tbsp applesauce plus 1 tbsp Prune Puree (page 42)
- 2 tbsp cream and ¼ cup (30 g) finely diced strawberries
- for older toddlers, 1 tbsp shredded apple plus 1 tbsp finely chopped raisins or dates

storage tip

Refrigerate cooked oatmeal for up to 5 days. Reheat in a saucepan over medium-low heat, adding a splash of water to loosen the cereal as needed. Or, sprinkle with water, cover, and reheat in the microwave for 1 minute.

basic brown rice

Like oatmeal, brown rice is a useful staple that you can cook in batches to last for several days. Brown rice retains the hull and most of the rice's nutrients—a good range of minerals, vitamins, and iron. Offer it now and get your baby accustomed to its nutty flavor and chewy texture, and you may have luck getting it to stick.

1 cup (7 oz/220 g) brown rice

2 cups (16 fl oz/ 500 ml) low-sodium chicken broth or water

stir-ins (optional; see ideas at right)

1 In a medium saucepan over high heat, combine the rice and broth. Bring to a boil, stir, cover, and reduce the heat to low. Cook until the liquid is absorbed and the rice is tender, about 50 minutes or according to the package directions.

2 Remove from the heat and let stand, covered, for 5 minutes. Uncover and fluff the rice with a fork. If needed, pulse the cooked rice in a food processor or blender, adding 1/4 cup (2 fl oz/60 ml) water to prevent sticking and make a smooth puree. (The rice will be sticky, but a stir-in will loosen it up.) As your baby nears the age of 1, she may be ready to eat the grains whole.

3 Stir in flavorings, if desired. Check the temperature and serve.

mama on the go

No time to cook brown rice? That's okay; try this:

- Keep a box of instant brown rice in the pantry.

- Stock up on precooked brown rice bowls that you can heat in the microwave.

- Order extra brown rice next time you get Chinese takeout. Many restaurants offer a choice of white or brown rice.

stir it in

Here are some flavor variations for a single 1/2-cup (2 1/2-oz/75-g) portion:

- 2 tbsp Apple Puree (page 29) plus 2 tbsp First Chicken (page 53) and 1 tsp olive oil

- 2 tbsp Creamy Pear with Spinach (page 73) plus 2 tbsp First Beef (page 71) and 1 tsp olive oil

- 2 tbsp finely chopped mango, 2 tbsp rinsed canned black beans (mashed as needed), 1 tsp lime juice, and 1 tsp olive oil

the global baby

For decades, American parents were told that a baby's first meals should be bland. Ideally, the advice went, it should be plain rice cereal. But how does this compare with what babies are eating internationally? A quick world tour of baby food may surprise you with its variety.

beyond rice cereal

African babies are often started on meat, Japanese babies on fish. In India, babies are fed a mixture of rice and lentils flavored with yogurt, cumin, and mustard, with vegetables, meat, or fish added. Chinese babies enjoy congee, a smooth rice porridge often mixed with steamed fish. In Vietnam and Thailand, parents offer small portions of curry to babies. South American babies eat corn, beans, and tortillas. North African babies like hummus (chickpea, sesame, and garlic puree). Some French infants feast on tomatoes and artichokes.

A bland diet early on can be detrimental to a child's palate later.

brain foods

In the first year, your baby's tastes are forming and the brain is growing quickly. It's the perfect time to develop your child's appreciation of these brain-nourishing foods:

1 Salmon
2 Eggs
3 Avocados
4 Yogurt
5 Coconut
6 Flaxseed
7 Seaweed

go for flavor

There's no evidence that well-flavored food with interesting ingredients is harmful to babies. Indeed, a bland diet during the early months can be detrimental to a child's palate later on. The first year of life is a sensitive period in learning to accept new foods and flavors. When a variety of flavors are not introduced by age 1, chances are that person will prefer a blander and more limited diet into adolescence and adulthood.

Babies develop surrounded by the food culture of their mothers. Even before birth, the amniotic fluid that envelops a fetus is flavored by what the mother eats. Later, breastfed babies get a taste of their mamas' meals—especially distinctive flavors like mint, vanilla, and garlic—through the breast milk. When babies finally begin to eat solid foods, they show a marked preference for the flavors they experienced during these earliest months.

thicken it up

A delay in introducing lumpy, textured foods can lead to later picky eating. As soon as baby gets the hang of eating solid food, start introducing thicker purees, and then finger foods once you see the readiness signs (see page 64).

(see page 64)

custards & creams

The English have a beloved tradition of "nursery puddings," or custards and creams for small children. Rice pudding and bread pudding have traveled far, but roly poly pudding, whim wham, spotted dick, and chocolate puddle remain quintessentially British. Across the Channel, French tots are entranced by *oeufs à la neige*—meringue eggs floating on a lake of custard.

> The amniotic fluid that envelops a fetus is flavored by what the mother eats.

what do babies want?

In the 1920s, a physician named Clara Davis conducted an experiment with orphaned infants to find out. Over the course of several months she offered 35 simple, unprocessed foods to 15 babies and let them create their own meals, with no interference from adults. The babies often chose strange pairings, such as a breakfast of liver and orange juice and a dinner of eggs and banana. But every baby unerringly chose a well-balanced diet and grew up into a healthy young child—even those who had been sickly as infants. Not one baby chose a bland, mostly cereal-and-milk diet; no baby ate the same foods every day; and no baby chose quite the same diet as another.

hummus

10 minutes

freezer safe

makes about
2 cups
(16 fl oz/500 ml)

You may be surprised at how much your baby relishes this savory spread made from chickpeas (also known as garbanzo beans). Many moms report that it's a favorite food at this age! Serve hummus with small pieces of pita or other bread. Hummus freezes well for up to 6 months, so you can always have it on hand.

one 15-oz (470-g) can chickpeas or white beans, rinsed and drained

2 tbsp olive oil, plus more as needed

1 clove garlic, pressed

1/3 cup (3 1/3 oz/ 100 g) tahini (optional)

1 lemon

1 tbsp chopped fresh parsley (optional)

1 In a food processor or blender, combine the chickpeas and 3 tbsp water. Puree until smooth.

2 Add the olive oil, garlic, and tahini, if using. Cut the lemon in half and add the juice from one half. Process to mix. Taste and adjust the flavor and consistency with more lemon juice or olive oil.

3 Transfer to a bowl and sprinkle with the parsley, if using, before serving.

4 To store, refrigerate in an airtight container for up to 1 week, or spoon into ice-cube trays or other freezer containers and freeze, covered, for up to 6 months.

tahini

If you have trouble finding tahini at your local market (in the ethnic food aisle or near the peanut butter), look for it online. A paste made from sesame seeds, it can be used on toast like peanut butter, or in other Middle Eastern recipes, such as baba ganoush.

roasted red pepper dip

5 minutes

makes about
½ cup
(4 fl oz/125 ml)

Babies in this age group are really into finger foods. This pale orange dip, rich in vitamins A and C and immune-boosting antioxidants like beta-carotene and lycopene, makes a perfect snack when smeared on pita strips or bits of rice cake. Even if your baby can't dip on his own, with a little help he'll be highly entertained.

½ cup (3 oz/90 g)
jarred roasted red
bell peppers,
drained

2 to 3 tbsp (1 to
1½ oz/30 to 45 g)
fresh goat cheese
(pasteurized)

1 pita bread

1 Pat the peppers dry and puree in a food processor or blender until smooth. Add the goat cheese and puree until the mixture is well blended and creamy.

2 Cut the pita bread into narrow wedges or tiny triangles that your baby can handle. Dip the strips into the puree and serve, or let older babies try dipping on their own.

roasting peppers

Preheat the broiler. Halve fresh pepper(s) lengthwise and place cut side down on a foil-lined baking sheet. Place under the broiler about 4 in (10 cm) from the heat source. Broil until the skin is blackened, about 10 minutes. Remove and tent with foil. When cool enough to handle, pull out the membranes and seeds, peel the peppers, and slice.

storage tip

Refrigerate in an airtight container for up to 5 days.

banana & avocado guacamole

5 minutes

freezer safe

makes ½ to 1 cup
(4 to 8 fl oz/
125 to 250 ml)

Sounds like a wacky combination? It might, until you consider that both bananas and avocados are tropical fruits, both have smooth textures, and neither is too sweet. In fact, bananas' cousins plantains are commonly used in savory Caribbean dishes. If you like, you can even make this guacamole with 2 bananas only!

1 ripe avocado

1 banana

½ to 1 clove garlic

fresh lemon or lime juice, as needed

crackers or toasted pita triangles for serving

1 Halve the avocado and remove the pit. Scoop the flesh into a bowl.

2 Peel the banana, break the fruit into small chunks, and add it to the bowl with the avocado.

3 Press the garlic clove with a garlic press and add to the bowl, then sprinkle with a little lemon juice. Use a potato masher to mash and combine the fruits to the texture your baby prefers. Serve at once with crackers.

spice it up

Once your baby is accustomed to this dish, try mixing in a little chopped fresh or dried cilantro. People are born with a predisposition to either like its taste or not, so you'll find out quickly what your baby thinks. If cilantro is a no-go, try mint.

storage tip

Both avocado and banana flesh turn brown when exposed to air. It's not exactly appetizing, but it's not harmful either. You can keep this puree for up to 2 days in the fridge, and it freezes surprisingly well in an ice-cube tray for up to 3 months. In either case, minimize browning by pressing plastic wrap directly onto the food surface to lessen the exposure to air.

eggplant dip

50 to 55 minutes
(mostly hands-off)

makes 2 cups
(16 fl oz/500 ml)

Fresh mint and lemon juice add bright flavor to rich, meaty eggplant in this recipe. Eggplant dips are enjoyed all around the Mediterranean, especially during the summertime. If you have the grill fired up, try making this with a couple of grilled slender Italian eggplants. The smoky flavor added by the grill is a definite bonus.

1 medium globe eggplant

3/4 cup (6 oz/ 185 g) plain yogurt, preferably thick Greek-style

2 tbsp chopped fresh mint or parsley

2 tbsp fresh lemon juice

pita bread for serving

1 Preheat the oven to 375°F (190°C). Line a baking sheet with foil.

2 Trim the stem from the eggplant and place the eggplant on the prepared baking sheet. Roast until the eggplant is very tender when pierced with the tip of a knife and the flesh feels soft enough to scoop from the skins, 45 to 50 minutes. Put the eggplant in a paper bag to cool. When cool enough to handle, peel away the skin and coarsely chop the flesh. Puree the eggplant in a food processor or blender until smooth. You will have about 1 cup (8 fl oz/250 ml) puree.

3 In a large bowl, whisk the yogurt until smooth and add the eggplant puree, mint, and lemon juice. Cut the pita bread into narrow strips for dipping, and serve with the dip.

4 To store, refrigerate in an airtight container for up to 5 days.

yogurt tips

If thick Greek-style yogurt is unavailable, you can use plain whole-milk yogurt. Use the creamy top layer, if possible, since this part will be thick like Greek yogurt. Yogurt with a thinner consistency will work just as well for a dip if you can't get a thicker one.

peach & cherry smoothie

5 minutes

makes 2 cups
(16 fl oz/500 ml)

Once you have the basics down, you can make a smoothie using any kind of fruit (or vegetable!) your baby likes. For starters, carrot juice can take the place of the typical orange juice. Smoothies make a smart and easy breakfast for moms as well. We can all drink to that!

1 cup (6 oz/185 g) frozen peach slices

1 cup (6 oz/185 g) frozen cherries

1/2 cup (4 fl oz/ 125 ml) carrot or orange juice

1 cup (8 oz/250 g) plain yogurt

1 In a blender or food processor, combine the peaches, cherries, and juice. Puree until smooth.

2 Add the yogurt and blend again until smooth.

3 Pour into a sippy cup or glass and serve.

winning substitutions

- **for the fruit** choose frozen banana (place whole in the freezer and ignore the blackened skin), frozen mango, frozen mixed berries, chunks of fresh, canned, or frozen pineapple, or a combination

- **for the plain yogurt** choose vanilla yogurt, or for a thinner texture try milk, soy milk, rice milk, or almond milk

- **for the juice** choose antioxidant-rich pomegranate, blueberry, or Concord grape juice

big kid cups

From the age of 9 months and up, let your baby practice taking sips from a regular cup or glass—with hands-on help from you. A smoothie is a perfect practice beverage since it doesn't flow too quickly.

feeling sneaky?

Blend in a small handful of drained and squeezed thawed frozen spinach. The dark red cherry specks in this smoothie camouflage it, and the taste won't be detectable. Blueberries can also provide silmilar cover.

breakfast polenta

You might think of polenta (ground cornmeal) as a dinner side dish, but it makes a wonderful breakfast porridge. Fine-ground polenta cooks very quickly and has a smooth texture. Once your child turns 1, try cooking the polenta in milk instead of water for extra richness and flavor.

⅓ cup (2⅓ oz/ 75 g) fine-ground yellow polenta

pinch of salt

heavy cream for serving (optional)

fruit or savory toppings for serving (optional; see ideas at right)

brown sugar for serving (optional)

1 In a heavy saucepan over high heat, bring 1 cup (8 fl oz/250 ml) water to a boil. Whisk in the polenta, stirring constantly, and cook, stirring, until the polenta is the consistency of very thick cream, about 5 minutes.

2 Stir in the salt and let cool slightly. Ladle into a bowl and serve with cream, a fruit or savory topping, and/or brown sugar, if using.

fruit & savory toppings

- mashed raspberries or blackberries
- finely diced peaches or plums
- sugar-free applesauce
- finely chopped dried fruits
- poached eggs
- shredded Cheddar cheese
- finely chopped sun-dried tomatoes

storage tip

You can refrigerate cooked polenta for up to 5 days. To reheat, sprinkle with water, cover, and warm in the microwave for 30 seconds or 1 minute.

green beans & silken tofu

10 minutes

freezer safe

makes 1 cup
(8 fl oz/250 ml)

Add this puree to your baby's brown rice bowl for a delicious and nutritious meal. Cooked green beans and silken tofu both make terrific finger foods when your baby is ready to try them. Cut green beans into thin pieces on the diagonal, and cut the tofu into small chunks (pinky-fingernail size) or strips.

one 8 to 10 oz (250 to 315 g) package frozen green beans

1 tbsp olive oil

2 tbsp silken tofu

dash of low-sodium soy sauce

1 cup (5 oz/155 g) cooked brown rice (optional)

1 Bring a saucepan of water to a boil over high heat. Add the beans and return to a boil. Cover and cook until very tender and bright green, about 5 minutes. Drain the beans and rinse them under cold running water to stop the cooking.

2 Puree the beans with the olive oil in a food processor or blender until smooth. Measure out 1/4 cup (2 fl oz/60 ml) and freeze the remainder for a later use (see directions below). Add the tofu and stir to blend. Season to taste with the soy sauce. Check the temperature and serve, stirred into brown rice, if using.

3 To store, refrigerate in an airtight container for up to 5 days, or spoon into ice-cube trays or other freezer containers and freeze, covered, for up to 6 months.

start fresh

You can use trimmed fresh green beans for this recipe. Slender French beans (haricots verts) give the puree an especially nice texture. Cook fresh green beans for 7 to 9 minutes, or haricots verts for 5 to 6 minutes.

pasta stars with tomato sauce

This quick and flavorful tomato sauce can be doubled as needed and used in other recipes—see Pizza Bagels (page 136) and Baked Spinach & Cheese Pasta (page 138). The sauce is also a good vehicle for "hiding" vegetables. Stir in some cooked chopped spinach, or sauté diced carrots along with the shallot.

2 tsp olive oil

¼ cup (1½ oz/ 45 g) grated shallot or onion

1 clove garlic, minced or pressed

1 tbsp tomato paste

¼ tsp dried oregano

one 28-oz (875-g) can diced tomatoes

¼ to ½ lb (125 to 250 g) pasta stars, alphabet letters, or other tiny pasta shape

⅓ cup (1⅓ oz/40 g) ricotta cheese (optional)

1 In a large saucepan over medium heat, warm the olive oil. Add the shallot and cook, stirring constantly, until soft, 4 minutes. Add the garlic and cook, stirring, until fragrant, 30 seconds. Reduce the heat, add the tomato paste and oregano, and cook for 2 minutes more.

2 Increase the heat to medium-high, add the diced tomatoes with their juices, and bring to a boil. Reduce the heat to medium-low and simmer uncovered, stirring occasionally, until the tomatoes have broken down and the sauce is thick, about 20 minutes.

3 Meanwhile, bring a large pot of water to a boil over high heat and cook the pasta according to the package directions. Before draining the pasta, scoop out about ½ cup (4 fl oz/125 ml) of the cooking water.

4 Divide the sauce into portions to use now and store. Spoon one portion into freezer-safe containers, let cool, and freeze for up to 6 months. Add the drained pasta and ricotta to the pan with the remaining sauce. Toss, adding a splash of the reserved cooking water if needed to loosen the sauce. Check the temperature, and serve.

handy in the pantry

Two clever pantry items that will allow you to make tomato sauce on short notice are tomato paste in a tube and frozen diced shallot or onion, both of which keep for months. Check for these at well-stocked supermarkets.

baby's risotto with peas

25 minutes
(mostly hands-off)

freezer safe

makes 1¾ cups
(11 oz/345 g)

Traditional risotto is not hard to make, but it requires some attentive stirring; this streamlined version cuts out most of the labor for time-pressed moms. If you're cooking for your toddler, you can simply steam risotto rice to make a laid-back version of risotto that's creamier than regular rice.

1 cup (8 fl oz/ 250 ml) low-sodium chicken or vegetable broth

half a 5-oz (155-g) package frozen peas (about 1 cup)

½ cup (3½ oz/ 110 g) Arborio rice

1 tsp olive oil

2 tsp minced fresh mint or parsley, or 1 tsp crumbled dried

1 In a heavy-bottomed saucepan over medium-high heat, combine the broth, peas, rice, and olive oil. Bring to a boil, reduce the heat to low, cover, and cook, stirring once, until the liquid has been absorbed and the rice is thick and creamy, about 15 minutes.

2 Remove the saucepan from the heat. Stir in the mint, cover, and let stand for 10 minutes. Fluff the rice with a fork. If needed, puree the risotto in a food processor or blender or mash with a fork to a texture your baby can handle. Check the temperature and serve.

3 To store, refrigerate in an airtight container for up to 5 days, or spoon into ice-cube trays or other freezer containers and freeze, covered, for up to 6 months.

rice for risotto

Look for Arborio rice when making risotto. This medium-grain rice is starchier than regular long-grain rice and becomes creamy with cooking.

mac 'n' cheese with broccoli

25 minutes

makes 2 cups
(12 oz/375 g)

The all-purpose cheese sauce in this recipe can be put to use disguising any rejected vegetable you're hoping to get your child to eat. Use any cheese you like in place of the Cheddar: Swiss, jack, or even goat cheese. Similarly, any vegetable can stand in for the broccoli. Try cauliflower or peas.

1 cup (2 oz/60 g) broccoli florets

1 cup (3½ oz/105 g) elbow macaroni

2 tbsp unsalted butter

2 tbsp all-purpose flour

1 cup (8 fl oz/ 250 ml) whole milk, warmed slightly in microwave

1 cup (4 oz/125 g) shredded Cheddar cheese

pepper

1 Bring a large pot of water to a boil over high heat. Meanwhile, use kitchen shears to cut the broccoli into very small, equal-size pieces. Reduce the heat to medium-high and add the macaroni and broccoli. Simmer until the macaroni is just tender and the broccoli is tender but not mushy, 7 to 10 minutes. Drain and set aside.

2 Meanwhile, in a saucepan over medium heat, melt the butter. Reduce the heat to low, add the flour, and cook, stirring constantly, until the mixture is bubbly and golden, 2 minutes. Slowly whisk in the milk. Cook, stirring frequently, until the sauce thickens, 6 to 8 minutes. Gradually add the cheese and stir until melted.

3 Stir in the cooked pasta and vegetables, season with pepper, and serve at once.

storage tip

Refrigerate for up to 5 days. You can make up extra sauce and keep a big jar in the fridge or freezer, ready to heat and top pasta or veggies.

small cubes of
cheese

well-cooked string
beans, cut into
tiny pieces

diced orange
segments

pb and banana
squares

small cubes of seedless
watermelon

bite-sized pieces of
breadsticks

diced ripe
avocado

chickpea
halves

diced kiwifruit

finger foods

A world of new possibilities opens up when your baby is ready for finger foods. Before age 1, cut foods into tiny pieces the size of your pinkie fingernail. Quarter grapes, dice cooked carrots, and break up crackers. Once she chews her snacks confidently (around age 1), cut foods into strips the size of her pinkie finger.

quick snacks

- scrambled eggs
- roasted sweet potato sticks
- tiny dice of kiwifruit, avocado, mango, or seedless watermelon
- cooked chickpeas or black beans, mashed or halved
- well-cooked string beans or carrots, cut into tiny pieces
- small cubes of string cheese
- fig bars, broken into pieces
- crackers or bread sticks, broken into pieces
- small pieces of citrus fruit
- cut-up pieces of toast with a thin spread of nut butter
- egg or tuna salad on whole wheat bread
- pitted olives, cut up
- bran muffins
- pita and hummus

quick tips

- Peel apples, peaches, and pears before dicing and serving; remove the membranes from oranges or grapefruits.
- Cook all vegetables, pasta, and beans until soft. You should be able to mash them easily with a fork. Let them cool.
- Dips and spreads (mashed sweet potatoes, cream cheese, fruit preserves) are a great way to sneak in extra nutrition. Make sure thick spreads are spread thinly.
- Don't worry if each and every item you feed your tot isn't superhealthy. Sometimes the taste and texture experience is more important; fruit gelatin, for example, is almost void of nutrition, but he'll love the texture.

chokables

We've said it before, and we'll say it again: Keep choking hazards out of your baby's pincer grasp. Turn to the beginning of this chapter (page 65) for a list of the top offending foods to watch out for. And the number one rule? Always watch your tot while he's eating any kind of finger food, even if it's something he's had a million times before.

little chicken dippers

20 minutes

makes 10 to 20
chicken strips
plus about 1 cup
(8 fl oz/250 ml)
yogurt dip

Like fast food chicken nuggets, these crunchy little tidbits are fun for little eaters. Unlike the drive-thru ones, you know exactly what goes into them because you make them yourself. They're not much trouble at all, and the yogurt-cucumber dipping sauce can also be used with Lamb Meatballs (page 97) or any grilled meat.

CHICKEN DIPPERS

vegetable oil spray

1 large egg

3/4 cup (3 oz/90 g) panko (page 98) or dried bread crumbs

1/2 lb (250 g) chicken tenderloins or boneless, skinless chicken breast, cut into thin strips

YOGURT DIP

1 cucumber, peeled

1 to 2 cloves garlic

1/2 tbsp olive oil

1 tsp fresh lemon juice

1 cup (8 oz/250 g) plain yogurt, preferably thick Greek-style

1 For the chicken dippers, preheat the oven to 400°F (200°C). Line a baking sheet with foil and spray with oil. Beat the egg lightly in a small bowl and put the panko in a large plastic bag.

2 Dip the chicken strips in the bowl of beaten egg and then transfer to the bag of crumbs, gently shaking to coat. Arrange the coated chicken strips on the prepared baking sheet without touching and, if desired, spray lightly with oil to encourage browning. Bake until the chicken is cooked through and the coating is crisp, 10 to 15 minutes, depending on the size of the strips.

3 Meanwhile, to make the dip, cut the cucumber into chunks. Combine it with the garlic in a food processor or blender and puree the cucumber to a texture your baby can handle.

4 In a bowl, combine the olive oil and lemon juice. Stir in the yogurt with a rubber spatula, mixing well. Stir in the cucumber mixture.

5 As needed, cut the chicken strips into narrower strips or smaller cubes that your baby can handle. When cool, serve with a small bowl of the dipping sauce. Store the chicken in the fridge for up to 3 days and the yogurt dip for up to 1 week. To reheat the chicken, warm in the microwave for 20 to 30 seconds and check the temperature carefully before serving.

mini meatballs

25 minutes

freezer safe

makes 45 to 50 mini meatballs

At 9 to 11 months, babies are exploring finger foods, and meatballs are a favorite. Once you have the basic method down, you can swap in different meats and flavorings as you like (see ideas at right). These delicious meatballs will work for the whole family, too.

olive oil spray

1 lb (500 g) ground beef or a mixture of beef and pork

½ cup (2 oz/60 g) fine dried bread crumbs

1 large egg, lightly beaten

¼ cup (2 fl oz/ 60 ml) whole milk

1 tbsp chopped fresh parsley, or ½ tbsp dried

1 clove garlic, pressed

1 Preheat the oven to 400°F (200°C). Line 2 rimmed baking sheets with foil and spray with oil.

2 In a large bowl, combine the beef, bread crumbs, egg, milk, parsley, and garlic. Using your hands, mix the ingredients until just blended. Be careful not to overwork. Scoop up rounded teaspoonfuls of the meat mixture, roll into mini meatballs, and set on the prepared baking sheets, spacing evenly.

3 Bake until the meatballs are browned and cooked through, 15 to 18 minutes. Let cool, cut into halves or quarters as needed for baby to manage them, and serve.

storage tip

Make a big batch of meatballs and freeze some for up to 6 months, so you have them handy anytime. Reheat in a 350°F (180°C) oven for 5 to 10 minutes.

lamb meatballs

In Step 2, use ground lamb in place of the ground beef and/or pork, and mint in place of the parsley. Serve the meatballs with Yogurt Dip (page 95) for dipping.

lemony chicken meatballs

In Step 2, use ground chicken (or ground turkey) in place of the ground beef and/or pork, lemon juice in place of the milk, and thyme in place of the parsley. Combine the bread crumbs with the lemon juice before adding the other ingredients. Serve the meatballs with a blend of apricot preserves and Dijon mustard to taste.

asian-style pork meatballs

In Step 2, use all ground pork in place of ground beef and/or pork, use fresh cilantro in place of the parsley, and use ground ginger in place of the garlic. Serve the meatballs with almond or peanut satay sauce (page 134) for dipping.

swedish meatballs

In Step 2, use dill in place of the parsley and serve the meatballs with lingonberry jam or blueberry preserves for dipping.

spaghetti & meatballs

In Step 2, use oregano in place of the parsley and serve the meatballs with pasta and your favorite jarred sauce.

hide some spinach

Thanks to its bitter flavor and slippery texture when cooked, spinach isn't always popular with the toddler set. To sneak a little into baby's food, simply puree some spinach and add 2 tbsp into any meatball mixture.

salmon patties

15 minutes

freezer safe

makes 6 patties

One of the trickiest things about eating enough fish every week is having to go and buy it fresh and then use it within a day. A busy mom can't always keep to such a tight schedule, and that's when canned fish comes to your rescue. It keeps nearly forever in the pantry. Serve these cute little patties warm or cold.

one 7$\frac{1}{2}$-oz (235-g) can boneless, skinless pink or red salmon

2 tbsp finely diced shallot or onion

1 large egg, lightly beaten

$\frac{1}{4}$ cup (1 oz/30 g) plus 2 tbsp panko or regular bread crumbs

2 tbsp canola oil

sugar-free applesauce or plain yogurt for dipping

1 In a large mixing bowl, flake the salmon, breaking it up with a fork and checking it for large bones. If you see smaller bones or skin simply mash them with the fork (they are edible).

2 Add the shallot, egg, and $\frac{1}{4}$ cup (1 oz/30 g) panko and mix well. Using your hands, roll the mixture into 6 little balls and flatten slightly to make patties. Dust lightly with additional panko.

3 In a frying pan over medium heat, warm the oil. When it is hot, add the salmon patties and cook until golden on the underside, about 2 minutes. Turn the patties and cook until the second side is golden, 1 to 2 minutes more. Transfer to paper towels to drain briefly, cut into halves or quarters, check the temperature, and serve alongside applesauce for dipping.

4 To store, refrigerate for up to 2 days or freeze for up to 3 months. To reheat, warm in the microwave for 20 to 30 seconds and check the temperature carefully before serving.

panko

Panko, or Japanese bread crumbs, can be found in well-stocked supermarkets, Asian groceries, or online. You can use also plain dried bread crumbs, but panko will give your patties such a light crunchiness that it's worth seeking them out. You may never go back to ordinary bread crumbs.

hard-cooked eggs

A boon to the busy baby on the go (and mom trying to keep up), eggs are highly nutritious, quick cooking, and delicious. The most basic version is the hard-boiled egg, which you can make in batches, store for a week in the refrigerator, and dole out as a snack or to round out a meal.

4 to 6 large or extra-large eggs

1 Put eggs in a single layer in a saucepan and add water to cover by 2 in (5 cm). Place over high heat and bring to a boil.

2 As soon as the water begins to boil, remove the saucepan from the heat. Cover and set a timer for 17 minutes. Fill a large bowl with ice water.

3 After 17 minutes, carefully transfer the eggs from the hot water to the bowl of ice water to stop the cooking. When cool enough to handle, tap the bottom of an egg against a counter to break it, peel, and serve (cutting in halves or quarters, or chopping up as needed so your baby can manage them). Refrigerate the others for up to 1 week.

variation: deviled eggs

These are a fun snack for a big playdate or birthday party. Deviled eggs are easiest to make with freshly cooked eggs, as they peel easily. Cook and peel 6 eggs as described above. With a sharp knife, cut each egg in half lengthwise. Separate the yolks and whites and put the yolks in a small bowl. Add a sprinkle of salt and pepper, 2 tbsp mayonnaise, and 1/2 tsp mustard. Mash the yolks and seasonings together until creamy. Spoon a dollop of the yolk mixture back into each egg white half, sprinkle each with a pinch of paprika, and serve.

what about cholesterol?

Don't stress about it. Infants actually need more cholesterol (and fat) than adults for their rapidly developing brains and organs. Breast milk, nature's infant formula, is high in cholesterol. Your baby can handle a whole egg every day.

baby bolognese

25 minutes
(mostly hands-off)

freezer safe

makes 2 cups
(16 fl oz/500 ml)

Here is a quick version of the classic meat ragù, which traditionally needs to simmer for several hours. If you need to hold the noodles after draining, toss them with a drizzle of olive oil to prevent sticking. This sauce goes well with polenta (page 86) as well as with noodles.

1 tbsp olive oil

1/4 cup (1 1/2 oz/ 45 g) frozen minced shallot

1 clove garlic, pressed

1 lb (500 g) ground beef

2 tbsp tomato paste

1/2 cup (4 fl oz/ 125 ml) low-sodium chicken broth

1/4 to 1/2 lb (125 to 250 g) dried pasta, such as fettucine

2 tbsp heavy cream

1 In a frying pan over medium-high heat, warm the olive oil. When the oil is hot, add the shallot and cook, stirring constantly, until soft, 2 to 3 minutes. Add the garlic and cook, stirring, until fragrant, 30 seconds.

2 Add the beef and cook, stirring, until browned, 4 to 5 minutes. Stir in the tomato paste and broth. Bring to a boil, cover, and reduce the heat to a simmer until the meat is cooked through and soft, 10 to 15 minutes.

3 Meanwhile, bring a large pot of water to a boil over high heat and cook the pasta according to the package directions. Before draining the pasta, scoop out about 1/2 cup (4 fl oz/125 ml) of the cooking water.

4 Remove the sauce from the heat and stir in the cream. Divide the sauce into portions to use now and to store. Spoon one portion into freezer-safe containers, let cool, and freeze for up to 6 months. If needed, transfer the remaining sauce to a food processor and puree to a consistency your baby can handle, adding a splash of pasta-cooking water. Use kitchen shears to cut the drained pasta into small pieces, toss the pasta with the sauce, check the temperature, and serve.

french toast bites

10 minutes

makes 1 French toast sandwich

For your baby's first French toast, try a thin-sliced soft sandwich bread, white or wheat. Leave the bread out on the counter overnight to dry it, or toast it briefly, just to help it soak up more egg. Next time you have stale leftover bread, use it to double, triple, or quadruple this recipe as needed for the whole family.

1 large egg

1 tbsp whole milk

¼ tsp vanilla extract

2 tbsp almond or peanut butter

2 slices day-old (or lightly toasted) bread

1 tbsp unsalted butter

1 tbsp jam (optional)

1 In a pie pan or shallow bowl, beat the egg. Stir in the milk and vanilla and set aside.

2 Spread the nut butter on one slice of bread and press the bread slices together to make a sandwich. For a younger baby, prepare a single slice of French toast and spread with nut butter once cooked.

3 In a small frying pan over medium heat, melt the butter. While the butter melts, dip the sandwich in the egg mixture, turning it to soak both sides.

4 When the butter foams, put the sandwich in the pan and cook until nicely browned on the underside, 3 to 4 minutes. Turn and cook until the second side is browned, 3 minutes more.

5 Cut the sandwich crosswise into squares, diagonally into triangles, or into shapes with a small cookie cutter. Let cool slightly and serve with jam for dipping, if desired.

nut butters

If your family is allergy prone, consult with your pediatrician about when to introduce nut butters.

scalloped root vegetables

In this lighter version of scalloped root vegetables, the usual cream is replaced with broth. If you are feeling luxurious, use cream or half-and-half instead once your baby is old enough. For the vegetables, choose from potatoes, sweet potatoes, rutabagas, parsnips, turnips, or a colorful mixture.

2 to 3 root vegetables (see recipe note)

1 tbsp unsalted butter

2 cloves garlic, minced

1 tbsp flour

1 cup (8 fl oz/ 250 ml) low-sodium chicken or vegetable broth, warmed

1 tsp fresh thyme leaves, or 1/2 tsp dried

pepper

1 cup (4 oz/125 g) shredded Cheddar cheese

1 Preheat the oven to 375°F (190°C). Peel the vegetables and slice them thinly with a sharp knife, ideally 1/8 in (3 mm) thick. Layer the slices in a pie dish. (They will cook down a bit.)

2 In a saucepan over medium-high heat, melt the butter. Add the garlic and cook until fragrant, 15 to 20 seconds. Stir in the flour and brown for 30 seconds, stirring constantly. Add the stock and stir to combine well. Bring to a simmer and add the thyme and pepper.

3 Pour the broth over all the layered vegetables. Sprinkle the cheese over the top. Cover with foil and bake until the vegetables are tender, 35 to 40 minutes. Remove the foil, raise the heat to 400°F (200°C), and bake until the cheese is browned and bubbling, about 15 minutes longer. Let rest for 10 minutes before serving.

broiled tropical fruit salad

15 minutes

makes 3 cups
(18 oz/560 g)

Tropical fruits pair together naturally, and they taste great grilled. Here's an even easier way to get that summertime grilled flavor: just pop the fruits under the broiler to warm them and caramelize the top. Look for thick, translucent coconut cream in the drinks aisle of the supermarket.

1 cup (6 oz/185 g) pineapple cubes

1 cup (6 oz/185 g) mango cubes

2 bananas

2 kiwifruits, peeled

1 lime

1 tbsp sugar, preferably raw (optional)

coconut cream or plain yogurt for serving (optional)

1 Preheat the broiler.

2 Dice the pineapple, mango, bananas, and kiwifruits into a size that your baby can handle.

3 Combine all the prepared fruit in a square baking pan and shake the pan to spread it out. Squeeze the lime over the fruit and sprinkle with the sugar, if using.

4 Slip the dish under the broiler. Broil until the fruit is golden brown and caramelized, about 5 minutes.

5 Let cool, top each serving with a dollop of coconut cream or yogurt, if desired, and serve.

family fare

This sweet and lively cooked fruit makes a delicious dessert topping. Try it over coconut sorbet or vanilla ice cream, or with angel food cake or pound cake.

time saver

To make this easy dish even quicker, look for precut fruit in the produce department. Or, use thawed frozen or canned pineapple or mango. You can use any combination of fruit or even all one fruit.

mealtime

12 to 18 months

feeding a 12- to 18-month-old

Your baby's not a baby anymore! She's a toddler, with a mind of her own and energy to spare. Trying to get her to pause for a meal might be tricky. Meals may even start to become battlegrounds, with your little princess playing with her food or refusing to eat. The secret to keeping the peace? Don't engage.

healthy snacking

Some children eat just a small amount at meals, preferring to "graze" or snack steadily throughout the day. This can be a healthy pattern if the between-meal foods are healthy. Supermarket shelves overflow with unhealthy snacks for children—heavily sweetened or overly processed foods. While your baby is still too young to be influenced by peer pressure, avoid these kinds of snacks and offer the same kinds of wholesome foods you serve at meals.

how to start

Offer a variety of healthy foods at mealtime 3 times a day. A rough guide to the amount she'll now eat in a day: 4 to 8 tbsp of fruits and vegetables, 4 servings of breads and cereals (a serving is $1/4$ slice of bread or 2 tbsp of rice, pasta, or cereals), and 2 tbsp of protein, such as meat or poultry. Offer healthy snacks twice a day at predictable times, halfway between meals. Good choices include fruit, string cheese, small cups of yogurt, and whole-wheat crackers.

how to progress

If you haven't already, give your child a toddler fork and spoon. He'll probably have an idea of how to use them because he's been watching you. He'll have the most success at first with sticky foods like mashed potatoes. Anticipate some frustration and messes, but your tot will enjoy being treated like a big kid.

what to watch for

Don't be alarmed if your baby goes on a food jag (only pasta and peas, no fruit for days). The phase will pass. Also, around the first birthday, growth tends to slow down a bit, so you can expect your little one's appetite to decrease as well. Try to provide balanced nutrition over the course of a week, rather than focusing on each day or each meal. As long as the doctor says she is growing and thriving, you can trust your child to eat as much as she needs.

what to skip

You may love your afternoon soda but you know to avoid sharing it with your baby. Be just as cautious with foods loaded with trans fats or sugar. By choosing healthy foods for your baby now, you'll teach her to prefer them later in life.

bye-bye ba-ba

Easier said than done, in many cases. The American Academy of Pediatrics (AAP) recommends losing the bottle by now, but plenty of kids hang on till 18 months or even 2 years. If your baby is still clinging tenaciously to her ba-ba, here are a few ideas for easing the transition:

- Reserve bottles for the pre-bedtime feeding only.
- Use sippy cups with a soft nipple-like tip if your toddler seems reluctant to try the hard ones.
- Put breast milk or formula in the cup to break any "only from the nipple" association.

transition to table foods

Some 1-year-olds love their purees and refuse to make the move to table food. To encourage a reluctant eater to make the transition, try the following:

- Offer a variety of tidbits—avocado, cooked beans, rice, pasta, meat—at each meal. Let him explore and choose what he wants.
- Feed your toddler what you are eating yourself; she may be more interested in real food if she gets bites from your plate.
- Mix table food in with the baby food he's used to.
- Get into the habit of eating together with your toddler at least once a day, if possible. She'll feel like part of the family.

got milk?

After 1 year, cow's milk can replace formula or supplement nursing—up to about three 8-fl-oz (250-ml) servings a day. Choose whole milk, until 24 months, unless low-fat is recommended by the doc; fat is essential at this age for brain growth. (A family history of obesity may change this advice.) If you think your baby is drinking so much milk each day that he's not eating enough food, ask your doctor how much to give him.

the family table

Between commuting, cooking, dishes, bath, and bed, the evening hours are anything but relaxing for many parents. A new dilemma has arisen: Do you feed your baby early and eat with your spouse after the baby is in bed? Or do you give your tot a snack to tide him over until a proper family dinner later?

When your baby was still too young to eat solid food, or much of it, you may have enjoyed her presence at the dinner table as a calm observer. Now that your tot eats regular foods, you can finally have a real dinner together—except the fun may last about five minutes before she is ready to move on to the next activity. Plus, she may be hungry before your usual dinnertime, and she's not prepared to wait.

There's no right way to eat dinner— but you do have a right to enjoy it!

the new witching hour

Experts and parents agree there is more than one strategy for surviving—and possibly even enjoying—dinnertime. You can choose the tack that's right for your family. The only ground rule: At 5 P.M. every day, take a deep breath and give yourself a break. Don't set your expectations too high; you're doing the best you can, and quite frankly, you deserve a medal just for trying. What follows are three different ways families approach the dinner hour. Be flexible: As your baby grows older, you may try all three, or you may use different strategies on different nights. There's no right way to eat dinner—but you do have a right to enjoy it!

no time to cook

Sometimes, the easiest way to ensure a family dinner is to cook the meal ahead of time. Use Sunday night to prepare a favorite stew, casserole, or pasta dish generous enough to cover two meals during the week. You can also designate one night as healthy takeout night—pick up a rotisserie chicken and salad on your way home. And keep quick dinner staples like turkey meatballs, ravioli, frozen vegetables, and deli meat on hand so all you have to do is "assemble" dinner.

strategy 1: feed your baby first

Serve dinner to your baby early; after she's in bed, sit down and eat dinner with your partner. Who does it work for? Families in which one parent gets home from work closer to your baby's bedtime than to her dinnertime. The late-coming spouse can focus on playing with the baby instead of rushing through a meal; then, one parent can cook while the other puts baby to bed, or both parents can put the baby to bed and then cook together. This way, parents can enjoy a calm meal (maybe even over a bottle of wine!) without having to dodge flying food.

strategy 2: everyone eats together

Serve a single, traditional family dinner. Who does it work for? Families in which both parents (and any older kids) are home when your baby is hungry. Or, for those with busy workweeks, try it on the weekend. Your tot may be keener on trying new foods if he sees you enjoying them. For many parents, the challenge is keeping their tykes amused while they prepare dinner. Try putting your little one in a high chair in the kitchen to eat cereal and keep an eye on you; for older kids, offer an art project. This option, of course, doesn't allow you to savor the meal as much as with Strategy 1—you're too busy refilling sippy cups and cutting up food. But you do get to have a family dinner together.

strategy 3: your baby eats twice

Feed your tot a snack or part of his dinner at 5 P.M.; serve the rest when you and your spouse sit down later to eat. Who does it work for? Families in which the baby eats mostly table food and has a later bedtime. On nights when the dinner gets pushed back too late for your baby to wait, Junior can enjoy a bedtime snack while grownups dine.

the family who eats together

The daily struggles that have begun (or may begin soon) with your hard-headed tot are like a little preview of the teen years. But eating regular meals together as a family is one of the best investments you can make toward your older child's well-being. Teenagers in families who eat together are less likely to smoke, drink, take drugs, get depressed, or develop an eating disorder. They are also more likely to excel in school, eat their vegetables, and learn big words.

frittata

30 minutes
(mostly hands-off)

makes 1 frittata

Frittata is more than just a great finger food for baby. It's a quick and easy supper for the whole family. The endlessly adaptable frittata can serve as a vehicle for any cooked or quick-cooking vegetables or meat you care to add. It's delicious served warm or at room temperature with a green salad and cold cuts.

butter for pan

6 large eggs

1 tsp minced fresh or 1/2 tsp dried herbs (optional; see ideas at right)

salt and pepper

1 to 2 tbsp olive oil

1/2 cup (3 oz/90 g) grated shallot or onion

1 cup (4 to 5 oz/ 125 to 155 g) vegetables and/or meat stir-ins (optional; see ideas at right)

1/3 cup (1 1/3 oz/ 40 g) grated Parmesan cheese, plus additional cheese (optional; see ideas at right)

1 Preheat the oven to 350°F (180°C) and set a rack in the upper third of the oven. Butter a pie dish. In a mixing bowl, whisk together the eggs, herb, if using, and salt and pepper to taste. Set aside.

2 Heat a frying pan over medium heat. Add 1 tbsp olive oil, or 2 if you have stir-ins to cook as well. Add the shallot and cook, stirring, until translucent, about 2 minutes. Add the vegetables and/or meat, if using, and sauté for 2 minutes to warm through (or a few minutes longer to soften uncooked vegetables, such as bell pepper).

3 Transfer the vegetables and/or meat to the buttered pie dish and shake to distribute them evenly. Pour in the egg mixture and sprinkle with the cheese. Bake until the center is set and the edges are browned and pulling away from the sides, about 15 minutes. After cooking, let stand for 5 minutes. Use a thin spatula to loosen the frittata from the pan, then cut into wedges or smaller pieces that your child can handle. Serve warm or at room temperature.

stir it in

- rosemary, sage, thyme, or basil
- thawed frozen hash-brown potatoes or mixed diced vegetables
- diced zucchini, tomatoes, and/or bell pepper
- diced ham, pancetta, or precooked sausage
- shredded Swiss or Cheddar or crumbled feta or goat cheese

omelet

Not just for breakfast, an omelet can be a lifesaver when you have a starving toddler and no dinner plan. Check the fridge for some leftover vegetables you can dice, heat, and fold into the middle to round out this dish into a meal. Grown-ups can enjoy their dinner omelets with a glass of chilled white wine.

2 large or extra-large eggs

salt and pepper

2 tsp unsalted butter

minced fresh vegetables or herbs

grated or crumbled cheese (optional)

1 In a bowl, combine the eggs, 1 tbsp water, and salt and pepper to taste. Beat lightly with a fork just until the egg yolks and whites are combined. Have ready a serving plate and pan lid.

2 In an 8-in (20-cm) nonstick frying pan over medium-high heat, melt the butter. When it foams, swirl the pan to coat and pour in the eggs. With a heatproof rubber spatula, stir the eggs with small, circular motions until soft curds start to form, 30 seconds to 1 minute.

3 As the mixture firms, spread it evenly over the bottom of the pan; scrape down the sides of the pan as needed. Stop stirring the curds to let the omelet begin to firm up, and let it cook until almost firm, about 1 minute. (If cooking an omelet for a grown-up, cut this time in half for softer eggs.) If using additional ingredients, fold in now.

4 Remove the pan from the heat, cover with a lid or a plate, and let stand for 1 minute. Place the pan over low heat for 20 seconds. With the spatula, lift one side of the omelet and fold it in half. Slide the omelet out of the pan onto the serving plate. Cut the omelet into pieces your child can handle, and check the temperature before serving.

silky eggs

Using milk or cream rather than water to loosen the eggs gives an omelet a silky texture and also makes it harder to overcook the eggs. The same holds true for Scrambled Egg (page 60).

egg-in-the-hole

10 minutes

makes 1 serving

Egg-in-the-hole goes by a number of aliases, most of them fun—egg-in-a-basket, egg-in-a-boat, cowboy eggs, one-eyed toast—and it's simply the easiest way to cook and serve fried eggs and toast. Your child will appreciate this classic childhood comfort food more and more as she gets older.

1 slice sourdough, buttermilk, potato, or wheat bread

1 to 2 tbsp unsalted butter

1 large egg

salt and pepper

pinch of cinnamon sugar or paprika (optional)

1 With a biscuit cutter or the rim of a glass, cut a 2- to 3-in (5- to 7.5-cm) round from the center of the bread slice, reserving the round. Have a serving plate ready.

2 In a small nonstick frying pan over medium to medium-high heat, melt 1 tbsp of the butter. When it foams, place the slice of bread and the bread round in the pan.

3 Making sure there is plenty of butter underneath, carefully crack the egg into the hole in the bread and sprinkle with salt and pepper. Cook until golden brown on the bottom, 2 to 3 minutes. Add more butter as needed to brown and crisp the second side of the toast. Flip the bread and egg and the bread round. Cook until the yolk is set, 3 to 4 minutes more (if cooking for a grown-up, you can cut this time in half for a runny yolk).

4 Transfer the egg-in-the-hole and bread round to a plate and sprinkle with cinnamon sugar or paprika, if using. Let cool slightly and serve, cutting up the egg-in-the-hole for your baby as needed.

blueberry-oatmeal mini pancakes

These pancakes have just a pleasant hint of sweetness, mostly from the blueberries. Although not discernible, the oats boost the pancakes' nutrition. If you have whole-wheat flour on hand, use it in place of regular flour. If you can't find dried blueberries, use fresh ones, or try chopped raisins or other tiny pieces of dried fruit.

2 large eggs

1½ cups (12 fl oz/ 375 ml) milk

½ tsp vanilla extract

½ cup (1½ oz/45 g) quick-cooking oats

½ to ¾ cup (2 to 3 oz/60 to 90 g) dried blueberries

1¼ cups (6½ oz/ 200 g) all-purpose or whole-wheat flour

1½ tbsp baking powder

1 tbsp sugar

½ tsp salt

½ tsp ground cinnamon

vegetable oil spray for pan

warmed maple syrup for serving

1 Preheat the oven to 200°F (95°C) and place a baking sheet or oven-proof platter on the middle rack.

2 In a bowl, lightly beat the eggs. Add the milk, vanilla, oats, and dried blueberries and stir to combine. Set aside.

3 In another bowl, sift or whisk together the flour, baking powder, sugar, salt, and cinnamon. Add the flour mixture to the egg mixture and stir with a wooden spoon until just combined.

4 Heat a griddle or large skillet over medium to medium-high heat. Spray the griddle lightly with oil. When the griddle is hot, spoon about 1 tbsp of the pancake mixture onto the griddle. Cook one pancake "for the pan" to get the temperature right before ladling more. Cook each pancake until bubbles form on the top and the underside is golden brown. (If you make rows of pancakes across the griddle, by the time you finish the last row, the first one will likely be ready to flip.) Flip each pancake with a thin spatula and cook until the second side is golden, just a minute longer. Transfer the finished pancakes to the oven to keep warm and repeat to make the remaining pancakes.

5 Cut the pancakes into small pieces as needed and serve with maple syrup. These freeze well for up to 6 months; reheat in the toaster. If your child is teething, give her a still-frozen one to gnaw on.

veggie pancakes

Potato pancakes are always popular, and they're a perfect way to work more colorful veggies into your baby's diet. If you can shred it on a box grater, you can use it in this recipe. Swap in unpeeled softer vegetables for the zucchini or peeled denser ones for the potato (see the suggestions on the facing page).

2 cups (10 oz/315 g) shredded russet potato, squeezed dry

1 cup (5 oz/155 g) shredded zucchini, squeezed dry

1/2 small onion, shredded, or 1/2 cup (3 oz/90 g) frozen diced onion

1 large egg, lightly beaten

1/4 cup (11/2 oz/45 g) all-purpose or whole-wheat flour, or as needed

1/2 tsp salt

1/4 tsp pepper

vegetable oil spray

applesauce and/or sour cream for serving

1 Preheat the oven to 200°F (95°C). Place a baking sheet or ovenproof platter on the middle rack.

2 In a large mixing bowl, combine the potato, zucchini, and onion and toss to mix. Stir in the beaten egg. Sprinkle the flour, salt, and pepper over the mixture and stir to combine. If the mixture does not hold together well, sprinkle in a little more flour.

3 Heat a large frying pan or griddle over medium heat. When it is hot, spray generously with oil. Using a large serving spoon, scoop about 2 tbsp pancake batter into your hand, flatten it as best you can, then put it in the pan and flatten with a large spatula. Cook the pancakes until nicely golden on the bottom, 2 to 4 minutes, then turn and cook on the second side until the underside is browned and the pancakes are cooked through, 2 to 4 minutes more. As the pancakes are cooked, transfer them to the oven to keep warm. Repeat to make the remaining pancakes.

4 Serve the pancakes, cut into wedges or strips your child can manage, with applesauce and/or sour cream.

storage tip

Once cooked, these vegetable pancakes freeze well. Wrap them in plastic or foil before sealing in a zippered plastic freezer bag. Thaw and crisp in a 350°F (180°C) oven for 5 to 10 minutes.

spinach-potato pancakes

In Step 2, use 1 box (10 oz/315 g) thawed spinach in place of the zucchini. Thaw the spinach in the microwave if needed, drain, and squeeze it dry in a clean kitchen towel or paper towels.

eggplant-potato pancakes

In Step 2, use a globe eggplant in place of the zucchini. Cut off the stem and shred the eggplant as you would the zucchini, then squeeze dry in a clean kitchen towel or paper towels.

carrot-zucchini pancakes

In Step 2, use 2 cups (10 oz/310 g) shredded carrots (about 4 large carrots) in place of the potato. You can leave the peels on if you like. Add a sprinkle of extra flour if needed to hold the pancakes together.

sweet potato pancakes

In Step 2, use a peeled and shredded sweet potato in place of the potato. Add a sprinkle of extra flour if needed to hold the pancakes together.

perfect pancakes

As a general rule of thumb when making potato pancakes, thinner is better and lower heat is better to help the pancakes cook through.

baked sweet potato fries

20 minutes

makes
6 to 8 servings

Here's a fry you can serve to your child without a twinge of guilt. Sweet potatoes are nutritionally flawless, and the oil used to cook these is heart- and brain-healthy olive oil. They don't cook up as crisp as French fries, but they sure are delicious. Serve them at a playdate and watch them disappear.

**¾ lb (375 g)
precut sweet
potato spears**

2 tbsp olive oil

1 tsp dried thyme

salt and pepper

1 Preheat the oven to 450°F (230°C).

2 In a bowl, drizzle the sweet potato spears with the olive oil. Using your hands, toss to coat the potatoes. Spread the spears in a single layer on a rimmed baking sheet and sprinkle with the thyme and salt and pepper to taste.

3 Roast, stirring with a spatula halfway through the baking time, until the potatoes are tender and brown at the edges, 15 to 20 minutes. Let cool slightly and serve.

start fresh

You can cut your own sweet potato spears. If you choose organic sweet potatoes, scrub them but don't worry about peeling them. Cut 1 or 2 sweet potatoes into slices ⅓ in (9 mm) thick, then cut each slice into spears ⅓ in (9 mm) wide and 3 in (7.5 cm) long.

storage tip

Refrigerate the sweet potato fries for up to 5 days. To reheat, crisp in a 350°F (180°C) oven for 5 to 7 minutes.

red beans & rice

25 minutes

makes 3 cups
(20 oz/625 g)

Beans and rice are favored foods for babies and tots all over Latin America and the Caribbean. Here, turkey sausage adds extra savory flavor. For variety, the same dish can be made with white beans and sage or with black beans and cumin in place of the kidney beans and thyme.

1 cup (7 oz/ 220 g) white or brown rice, instant if desired

olive oil spray

¼ lb (125 g) precooked turkey or chicken sausage, cut into thin rounds

¼ cup (1½ oz/ 45 g) grated shallot or onion

one 14-oz (440-g) can kidney beans, rinsed and drained

one 14½-oz (455-g) can stewed tomatoes

½ tsp dried thyme

1 Prepare the rice according to the package directions.

2 Meanwhile, spray a large frying pan with the oil and add the sausage. Place over medium heat. As the sausage begins to sizzle, stir occasionally until browned and heated through, 2 minutes.

3 Using a slotted spoon, transfer the sausage to a cutting board and set aside. When cooled, chop it up into a size your baby can handle. If there is less than 1 tbsp fat left behind in the frying pan, spray a little more oil. When the oil is hot, add the shallot and cook, stirring constantly, until translucent, 2 minutes.

4 Add the beans, tomatoes, and thyme and stir well. Bring to a boil, then reduce the heat to medium-low and simmer to blend the flavors, 4 to 5 minutes. When the rice is ready, stir it in and mix thoroughly. Mash as needed to a consistency your child can manage. Stir in the sausage, let cool, and serve.

5 To store, cover and refrigerate for up to 3 days.

minestrone

Minestrone is a classic farmhouse soup, essentially a vehicle for any leftovers that have accrued over the course of the week. You can use any vegetables you like; pasta or instant rice; beans or no beans. The hodgepodge of ingredients can lure little ones into eating veggies—of course, they may also flat out refuse!

2 tbsp olive oil

1 onion, grated in food processor

2 cloves garlic, grated in food processor

8 cups (64 fl oz/2 l) low-sodium chicken or vegetable broth

½ lb (250 g) egg noodles

one 14-oz (440-g) bag frozen vegetable medley (such as corn, peas, carrots, and green beans)

one 15-oz (470-g) can white navy beans, drained and rinsed

one 15-oz (470-g) can diced tomatoes

salt and pepper

1 In a large pot over medium-high heat, warm the oil. Add the onion and garlic and cook, stirring frequently, until translucent, 2 to 4 minutes.

2 Add the broth, increase the heat to high, bring to a boil, and add the noodles. Cook for 5 minutes.

3 Add the vegetable medley, beans, and tomatoes. Bring to a boil, then reduce the heat to medium and simmer the soup until the noodles are fully cooked and the flavors are blended, 5 to 7 minutes more. Season with salt and pepper, check the temperature, and serve.

4 To store, cover and refrigerate for up to 5 days.

family fare

If you like, top the minestrone with grated Parmesan cheese. Shredded roast chicken and chopped cooked sausages are two meaty stir-ins you can add to the finished soup to beef it up further. Warm a loaf of French bread in the oven or make garlic bread, toss together a green salad, and there you have Sunday dinner.

corn & red potato chowder

45 minutes

makes 4 cups
(32 fl oz/1 l)

Chowder is a hearty soup perfect for the first days of autumn. If you want to add protein, you can try shredded rotisserie chicken, or add chopped shrimp to simmer during the last few minutes of cooking. Or, if you like, chop 2 strips of bacon and add them to the pan along with the onion to add a smoky savor to the chowder.

1½ tbsp canola oil

1 onion, grated in food processor

2 cloves garlic, grated in food processor

½ lb (250 g) red potatoes (preferably organic), skins on, diced

2 cups (16 fl oz/ 500 ml) low-sodium chicken broth

salt and pepper

3 cups (24 fl oz/ 750 ml) whole milk

one 10-oz (315-g) package frozen corn kernels (about 2 cups)

2 tbsp all-purpose flour

2 tbsp unsalted butter, at room temperature

paprika (optional)

1 In a large pot over medium-high heat, warm the oil. Add the onion and garlic and cook, stirring constantly, until softened but not browned, 2 to 4 minutes.

2 Add the potatoes, broth, and salt and pepper to taste. Bring to a boil and reduce the heat to medium-low. Simmer until the potatoes are just tender, 20 to 25 minutes.

3 Put the milk and corn in a microwave-safe container and heat for 1 or 2 minutes to warm. Stir the warm milk and corn into the pot and return to a simmer. Meanwhile, in a small bowl, combine the flour and butter and mash together to form a paste. Slowly add the flour-butter mixture into the simmering soup, stirring until the butter is melted.

4 Simmer the chowder until thick, 3 to 5 minutes. Season to taste and transfer your baby's portion to a food processor or blender to puree briefly. Serve with a sprinkling of paprika, if desired. To store, cover and refrigerate for up to 3 days.

start fresh

To use fresh corn for this soup, you'll need 4 cobs. Stand each cob upright in a shallow bowl and use a small, sharp knife to slice the kernels from the core. Run the back side of the knife down the cob to squeeze out any extra corn juices and pour these into the soup, as well.

picky, picky, picky

Once children reach the age of 12 to 18 months, their willingness to try new foods may suddenly drop, usually ushering in a phase of picky eating. Parents of picky eaters often worry, but this is an extremely common phase that doesn't typically cause any health or developmental problems. Here's the low-down.

why picky eating happens

Just as you were congratulating yourself for teaching your baby to devour an impressive variety of foods, including spinach and broccoli, she suddenly turns the tables and just says no. Why?

- **Neophobia** Kids are naturally averse to trying unfamiliar foods thanks to this protective instinct. It emerges as toddlers become more mobile and able to stray from their parents' watchful eyes.

  - **It's turning into a game** If you spend a lot of energy coaxing a reluctant child to eat, he may start to enjoy that interaction and prolong the refusal for extra attention.

  - **It's turning into a battle of wills** If your child thinks she's found an area where she can exercise power over you, her stubbornness may increase, reinforcing the picky eating.

how to handle it

Take comfort: Most children outgrow the picky phase. Try not to get involved in battles over food. Accept the rejection when it happens, but keep offering a wide range of foods. Don't be shy about offering the same rejected foods over and over. As you continue to expose your tot to new foods (and eat them yourself), he'll become less afraid of the unfamiliar. Let your child touch or play with foods to get acquainted with them.

slip it in

If your toddler is simply boycotting vegetables, turn to pages 84, 97, and 118 for ways to sneak some veggies into your child's food and ensure he is getting all the nutrients he needs. But don't forget to keep offering these foods in their unadorned form. It can take 15 tries, or more, for a food to become familiar. That may mean offering them once a week for at least 4 months!

maximize your mealtime mom style

Every family handles mealtimes a little differently. One of the two approaches below will probably appeal more strongly to you—but see what you can learn from the other camp.

If this sounds like you: "I'm comfortable being the adult in charge. When I know what's best for my kid, there's no need to debate my decisions."

You're probably a: Benevolent Ruler

Your mealtime style: "No pussy-footing around: My kid's going to learn to eat what the family eats, even if it takes a lot of patience and repetition."

What to keep in mind: While you have every right to stand your ground and not become a short-order cook for your toddler, you may start to find yourself getting frustrated by his eating jags. In that case, sneaking a few veggies into the pasta sauce or muffins may help you keep up your patient smile. It's not a sign of weakness—just pragmatism!

If this sounds like you: "I want my child to learn to think for himself, so I give him a lot of autonomy both in general and at mealtime."

You're probably a: Laissez-Faire Mom

Your mealtime style: "I trust my child to eat the foods she needs. I'm taking the big-picture view of what she's eating every week."

What to keep in mind: Although a low-pressure approach at the table is good, don't forget to be persistent in offering rejected foods again and again. Even if you feel like a broken record, your efforts will help in the long run and keep you from sliding too far down the slippery path of least resistance!

thanks but no thanks

When your toddler refuses to eat a food, try not to force the issue. However, you can use your parental prerogative to request (with enthusiasm!) that your tot try just one bite of every food. Call it a "no-thank-you bite" or say, "It's all right! Just one bite!" You'll sometimes find that just one bite leads to more.

orzo & vegetables

Orzo is a fun pasta shape because it looks like grains of rice (or, technically, barley). If you can't find it, use any interestingly shaped pasta, such as bowties or corkscrews. Look for prepared pesto in a tube—it will keep for months in the fridge, while you just use a tablespoon or two at a time.

8 oz (250 g) orzo or other small shaped pasta

2 tbsp olive oil

one 10-oz (315-g) package frozen mixed vegetables (such as peas, carrots, green beans, and/or corn)

2 tbsp prepared pesto

pinch of salt

1/4 to 1/2 cup (1 to 2 oz/30 to 60 g) grated Parmesan cheese

fresh lemon juice as needed

1 Bring a large pot of water to a boil and cook the orzo according to the package directions.

2 Meanwhile, in a large frying pan over medium heat, warm the oil. Add the vegetables and cook, stirring often, until heated through, about 2 minutes. Reduce the heat to low.

3 Before draining the pasta, scoop out about 1/2 cup (4 fl oz/125 ml) of the pasta-cooking water. Add the drained pasta to the frying pan and add the pesto, salt, and cheese and a splash of the reserved pasta-cooking water. Stir over low heat until the cheese is melted and the flavors are blended. Drizzle with lemon juice to taste. Check the temperature and serve.

4 To store, cover and refrigerate for up to 5 days.

start fresh

Make your own pesto and freeze it in an ice-cube tray. In a food processor or blender, puree 2 garlic cloves and a small handful of pine nuts. Add the leaves from a large bunch of basil, puree, then stir in a handful of grated Parmesan cheese, a generous pour of olive oil, a pinch of salt, and a squeeze of lemon.

barley with butternut squash

Rice is nice, but barley is better. It may be something you never tried cooking before your little one arrived, but if you give this dish a try you will soon have the whole family loving it! With a nutty flavor and chewy texture, barley offers more nutrition and fiber than rice. See page 20 for directions on roasting the squash.

1 tbsp olive oil

½ onion, grated in a food processor

2 cloves garlic, pressed

½ lb (250 g) ground turkey

1 cup (7 oz/220 g) pearled barley

1½ cups (7½ oz/ 235 g) roasted squash cubes

1 tbsp tomato paste

pepper

2 cups (16 fl oz/ 500 ml) low-sodium chicken broth, or as needed

1 Preheat the oven to 350°F (180°C). Heat an ovenproof frying pan over medium-high heat and add the oil. When the oil is hot, add the onion and garlic and cook, stirring constantly, until soft, 2 to 4 minutes.

2 Add the ground turkey and cook, breaking it up with a wooden spoon and stirring often, until browned, 4 to 5 minutes. Add the barley, roasted squash, tomato paste, a sprinkling of pepper, and the broth. Stir to combine and cover with a lid or foil.

3 Put the pan in the oven and bake until the barley is tender (it will still be chewy), about 1 hour. Mash or cut the squash as needed to a consistency your child can manage. (You can also puree all or part of your baby's portion briefly in a food processor or blender with a splash of broth.) Check the temperature before serving.

storage tip

Refrigerate for up to 3 days. Reheat in a 350°F (180°C) oven for 10 minutes.

parmesan pasta

This recipe may actually be easier than opening a box of mac 'n' cheese. Because there are so few ingredients, it's worth getting a hunk of good imported Parmesan and grating it yourself while the pasta cooks. The peas and ham here are just yummy extras; if you don't have either handy, the cheese is delicious all on its own.

2 thin slices ham (optional)

1/2 lb (250 g) bowtie pasta

one 10-oz (315-g) package frozen peas (about 2 cups) (optional)

3 tbsp unsalted butter

1/2 tsp grated nutmeg

1 cup (4 oz/125 g) grated Parmesan cheese

salt and pepper

1 Bring a large pot of water to a boil over high heat. Meanwhile, cut the ham, if using, crosswise into thin strips.

2 Add the pasta to the boiling water and cook according to the package directions. After the pasta has cooked for about 5 minutes, add the peas, if using, to the pot with the pasta.

3 Before draining the pasta, scoop out about 1/2 cup (4 fl oz/125 ml) of the cooking water. Melt the butter in the pot; when it foams, add half to all of the reserved cooking water, depending on how loose you want your sauce. Cook briefly to reduce the water, then sprinkle with the nutmeg.

4 Add the pasta and peas, if using, to the pot, shake and swirl the pot to coat the pasta with the sauce, then add the Parmesan and strips of ham, if using. Season to taste with salt and pepper, toss, and check the temperature before serving.

5 To store, cover and refrigerate for up to 5 days.

cheese quesadillas

10 minutes

makes 2 to 4
quesadilla shapes

Not your average quesadillas, these open-faced sandwiches are made into super-cute shapes by using a larger cookie cutter for the tortilla and a smaller one (in the same shape, or a different one) for the cheese. Check your market for flavored tortillas in a rainbow of colors: green spinach, pink tomato, or blue corn.

**1 corn or flour
tortilla (preferably
whole wheat)**

**4 slices Monterey
jack or Cheddar
cheese**

olive oil spray

**mild salsa for
serving (optional)**

1 Using a large cookie cutter, cut out shapes from the tortilla as desired. Using a smaller cookie cutter, cut the cheese slices into an equal number of shapes.

2 Heat a frying pan with a lid over medium heat. Spray with olive oil and add the tortilla cutouts. Cook the first side until the underside is golden, 1 to 2 minutes. Flip the cutouts and top each with a cheese cutout. Cover the pan and cook on the second side until the cheese is melted, 1 to 2 minutes more.

3 Transfer the quesadillas to a plate and let cool slightly. If needed, cut into pieces small enough for your child to handle, garnish with the salsa, if using, and serve.

storage tip

Refrigerate for up to
2 days. Reheat in an
oil-sprayed frying pan over
medium heat just until
the cheese is melted.

tofu almond satay

Tofu is a vehicle for other flavors—here, a tasty almond sauce with Asian flair. If your baby has not yet tried nuts or soy, offer each alone for a few days and watch for a reaction before trying any other new foods. If your family is allergy prone, double-check with your doc about when to introduce nuts and soy.

1 lb (500 g) firm tofu

sesame oil for brushing

1/2 cup (5 oz/150 g) almond or peanut butter

2 tbsp fresh lemon juice

2 tbsp honey

2 tbsp low-sodium soy sauce

2 tbsp fresh ginger, peeled and chopped

2 cloves garlic, pressed

cooked rice or rice noodles for serving

1 Preheat the broiler and line a rimmed baking sheet with foil.

2 Pat the tofu dry and cut into slices 1/4 in (6 mm) thick. Arrange them on the prepared baking sheet and brush with sesame oil. Slip under the broiler about 4 in (10 cm) from the heat source and broil until browned and heated through, about 7 minutes.

3 Meanwhile, in a food processor or blender, combine the almond butter, lemon juice, honey, soy sauce, ginger, and garlic and blend until smooth. Pour into a saucepan over medium heat and warm until the sauce is heated through, about 5 minutes. Alternatively, pour into a microwave-safe bowl and cook on high heat for 2 minutes. (Stir well and check the temperature carefully before serving.)

4 Let the tofu and sauce cool slightly and cut up the tofu and noodles, if using, to a size your child can handle. Serve the tofu drizzled with the sauce over rice or noodles, or let your child dip the tofu in the sauce. The tofu can be stored in the refrigerator for up to 2 days. The sauce can be stored in the refrigerator for up to 5 days.

baby burritos

10 minutes

freezer safe

makes 6 burritos

These are great on-the-go meals—just be sure to bring along some extra wipes! Between the beans, cheese, and avocado, these packets include a nice range of protein, fiber, healthy fat (from the avocado), and nutrition. You can make a batch of burritos, freeze the extras, and have a quick meal on hand at all times.

one 15-oz (470-g) can vegetarian refried beans

3/4 cup (3 oz/90 g) grated Monterey jack or Cheddar cheese

3 tbsp chopped fresh cilantro

6 small 7-in (18-cm) flour tortillas, (preferably whole wheat)

1/2 large avocado (or 1 small), pitted, peeled, and mashed

1 In a microwave-safe dish or small saucepan, stir together the refried beans, cheese, and cilantro. Heat the mixture in the microwave in 30-second increments or in the saucepan over medium heat, stirring occasionally, just until the cheese is melted.

2 Divide the bean mixture evenly among the tortillas and spread it down the middle of each. Top with the mashed avocado. Let the bean filling cool before folding in 2 sides of each tortilla and rolling up the burritos. Serve, cutting up the burrito as needed for your child to manage it.

storage tip

Wrap the burritos individually in foil and seal in a large zippered bag in the freezer. To thaw the frozen burritos safely, place in the fridge overnight. Rewarm in a 350°F (180°C) oven for 10 minutes or in a microwave for 1 minute and check the temperature before serving.

pizza bagels

15 minutes

freezer safe

makes 4 pizza
bagels

You can add almost any topping you'd like to these cheesy little treats. Try finely diced pineapple, diced ham or salami, finely chopped sun-dried tomatoes, thawed frozen artichoke hearts, or finely sliced mushrooms. If you're in a big hurry, use jarred tomato sauce in place of the crushed tomatoes and oregano.

2 whole-wheat mini bagels, halved and lightly toasted

one 14^1/$_2$-oz (455-g) can crushed tomatoes

1 tsp minced fresh oregano, or ^{1}/$_2$ teaspoon dried

salt

^{1}/$_3$ cup (1 oz/30 g) shredded mozzarella cheese

topping of choice (optional; see note above for ideas)

1 Preheat the oven to 400°F (200°C) and set a rack in the top third of the oven. Arrange the bagel halves on a baking sheet.

2 In a bowl, stir together the crushed tomatoes and oregano to make a simple pizza sauce. Season with a pinch of salt. (Leftover pizza sauce can be frozen for up to 3 months. Divide into small portions for topping a mini bagel or two.)

3 Evenly spread the tomato sauce on each bagel half, then top with the cheese. If desired, add additional topping(s).

4 Bake until the cheese is melted and bubbly and any topping is heated through, about 10 minutes. Let cool, cut into pieces as needed, and serve.

baked spinach & cheese pasta

50 minutes
(mostly hands-off)

freezer safe

makes 1 casserole

This is the perfect pasta dish for a make-ahead family weeknight dinner. You can easily double this recipe and freeze one casserole for later. Thaw overnight in the refrigerator and reheat in a 350°F (180°C) oven for 15 to 20 minutes. Use your favorite store-bought marinara sauce or see page 88 for an easy recipe.

olive oil for pan

one 10-oz (315-g) package frozen chopped spinach

1/2 lb (250 g) uncooked pasta shells

2 eggs

1 cup (8 oz/250 g) ricotta cheese

1/4 tsp ground nutmeg

pepper

1 1/2 cups (12 fl oz/ 375 ml) marinara sauce

1 cup (4 oz/ 125 g) shredded mozzarella cheese

1/4 cup (1 oz/30 g) grated Parmesan cheese

1 Preheat the oven to 400°F (200°C). Grease an 8-in (20-cm) square baking pan or casserole dish with olive oil. Thaw the spinach in the microwave and squeeze it dry in a clean kitchen towel or paper towels.

2 Bring a large pot of water to a boil over high heat and cook the pasta according to the package directions. Drain.

3 Meanwhile, in a large bowl, whisk the eggs lightly. Add the spinach to the eggs along with the ricotta, nutmeg, and pepper to taste; stir to blend. Stir in the cooked pasta and 1/2 cup (4 fl oz/125 ml) of the marinara sauce until the pasta is well coated. Pour into the prepared dish. Spread the remaining 1 cup (8 fl oz/250 ml) marinara sauce over the pasta mixture. Sprinkle the mozzarella and Parmesan cheeses evenly over the top.

4 Bake, uncovered, for 20 minutes, until the cheese just starts to bubble. Once out of the oven, let stand for 5 to 10 minutes. Cut up the pasta as needed for your child to manage it, check the temperature, and serve.

shrimp cakes

30 minutes

makes 12 cakes

Frozen shrimp is a key pantry ingredient to keep on hand. Flash-frozen on board immediately after catching, they are often better in quality than some fresh ones at the market. Shrimp is a common allergen, so if your family is allergy prone, consult with your baby's doctor about when to introduce it.

1 lb (500 g) peeled and deveined frozen shrimp, thawed in the microwave or refrigerator

1 large egg, lightly beaten

2 tbsp minced fresh chives

2 tbsp fresh lemon or lime juice

1 tbsp Dijon mustard

salt and pepper

2 cups (8 oz/250 g) panko (page 98) or regular bread crumbs

2 tbsp canola oil, or as needed

1 Line a baking sheet with waxed paper. Remove the tails from the shrimp if needed, place the shrimp in a food processor, and coarsely chop. Add the egg, chives, lemon juice, and mustard, and season with salt and pepper. Pulse to blend. Add 1 cup (4 oz/ 125 g) of the panko and pulse to blend.

2 Form the shrimp mixture into 12 balls, then flatten slightly into cakes. Roll the shrimp cakes in the remaining 1 cup (4 oz/125 g) panko and place on the prepared baking sheet. Refrigerate for 10 minutes.

3 In a large, heavy frying pan over medium-high heat, warm the 2 tbsp oil. Working in batches to avoid crowding, fry the cakes, turning once, until cooked through and golden brown on both sides, about 6 minutes total. Repeat to fry the remaining cakes, adding more oil to the pan as needed.

4 Cut the shrimp cakes into wedges or pieces your child can handle. Let cool and serve. To store, refrigerate for up to 3 days.

dipping sauce

For a zesty dip, stir a squeeze of lemon or lime juice into a couple of tablespoons of prepared mayonnaise.

ham and cheese pinwheels

kiwi stars

bell pepper strips

edamame

oyster crackers

ideas for bento combinations

bento 1

ham and cheddar pinweels

kiwi stars

red, yellow, and orange bell pepper strips

oyster crackers

edamame

bento 2

pita wedges with nut butter and jelly

balls of melon, halved

sliced cherry tomatos and diced cucumber

pretzels or goldfish

chopped dried apricots or mango

bento 3

sliced hard-boiled egg

small cubes of cheese with crackers

diced plum or peach

celery sticks with nut butter and chopped raisins

bento box

Bento—which means "box lunch" in Japanese—is the art of making food look adorable. Traditional Japanese mothers spent their mornings laboring over little boxes of edible art for their children. Most modern moms don't have time for this, but the concept still translates into great ideas for toddler meals.

what's in a bento box?

- A bento box features small compartments to fill with an array of foods. Traditionally, a foundation of rice is rounded out with vegetables and a protein, but you can include any mix of foods you'd like.

- A bento box is supposed to be colorful. Preparing meals this way is a good reminder to offer a rainbow of foods.

- A bento box is an excellent way to turn whatever you have on hand in the fridge into a toddler-tempting lunch.

- A bento box—with its small portions of different foods that can serve as a snack, lunch, or just healthy options for grazing—lets your toddler eat in a natural pattern.

bento fillers

- pinwheel sandwiches: Roll ham and cheese, or a nut butter and jam, in a pita wrap and slice into small pieces

- fruit shaped with a cookie cutter

- little rolls of salami

- hummus or eggplant dip with pita triangles or cut-outs

- frittata wedges

- meatballs or shrimp cakes

- mini pancakes or cut-up waffles

- mini muffins

- oyster crackers or goldfish

toddler appeal

Ever versatile, a bento box can help with picky eating; an array of cute foods in kid-size portions can induce even the fussiest eater to try at least one bite. For added fun, you can use cookie cutters or molds to shape foods like mini-sandwiches, cheese slices, or sticky rice. Turn making lunch into an art project, and before long your little one will want to help!

mushroom & zucchini rice pilaf

25 minutes

makes 3 cups
(18 oz/560 g)

Pilaf is a smart way to cook up rice and vegetables together in the same pot for a wholesome baby meal. True pilaf requires precooking the rice in oil. This shortcut version uses instant rice, which is already precooked. Choose instant white or brown rice, as you like. This recipe doubles easily.

½ small onion

half a 10-oz (315-g) package cleaned mushrooms (about 1½ cups)

1 zucchini, cut into chunks

1 tbsp olive oil

pepper

1 cup (8 fl oz/ 250 ml) low-sodium chicken broth

1 cup (7 oz/220 g) instant brown or white rice

1 Grate the onion in a food processor or blender. Add the mushrooms and zucchini and finely chop.

2 In a large frying pan over medium-high heat, warm the olive oil. Add the onion and cook, stirring constantly, until translucent, about 2 minutes. Add the mushrooms and zucchini, season with pepper, and cook, stirring often, until their moisture has evaporated, 5 to 7 minutes.

3 Transfer the vegetables to a saucepan, add the broth and rice, and stir to mix. Bring to a boil, reduce the heat to medium-low, cover, and simmer for 5 minutes. Remove the pan from the heat and let stand, covered, for 3 minutes. Fluff with a fork, let cool slightly, and serve.

4 To store, cover and refrigerate for up to 3 days.

spice it up!

As your child grows older and can chew well, you can liven up this pilaf by stirring in chopped raisins or other tiny pieces of dried fruits; spices, such as ½ tsp garlic powder or ¼ tsp each cumin and coriander; and flaked almonds. Add the stir-ins along with the rice.

chicken & vegetable couscous

20 minutes

makes 6 cups
(36 oz/1.15 kg)

This dish can easily be spiced up to feed the whole family. Stir in a pressed clove of garlic and $1/2$ teaspoon each of coriander and cumin along with the couscous. Your baby will likely enjoy the full-flavored version, too. Don't be shy about adding spices to your baby's food!

2 tbsp olive oil, plus more for serving

1 small onion, grated in a food processor

one 8-oz (250-g) package precut fresh or frozen squash cubes

1 cup (5 oz/155 g) frozen peas

pepper

one 15–fl oz (470-ml) can low-sodium chicken broth

1 cup (6 oz/185 g) instant couscous

1 cup (6 oz/185 g) shredded cooked chicken

1 In a large frying pan over medium-high heat, warm the 2 tbsp olive oil. Add the onion and cook, stirring frequently, until translucent, 2 to 4 minutes. Add the squash and the peas, season with pepper, and cook, stirring often, for 2 minutes.

2 Pour the broth into the pan. Bring to a boil, cover, reduce the heat to medium-low, and simmer until the vegetables are tender, about 10 minutes. Raise the heat to bring the broth back to a boil, add the couscous, stir, and remove from the heat. Cover and let stand for 5 minutes.

3 Fluff the couscous. Spoon the mixture into bowls and top with the shredded chicken. Drizzle each serving with olive oil and serve.

storage tip

Refrigerate the couscous mixture with the chicken for up to 3 days, or without the chicken for up to 5 days.

baked fish with mango

20 minutes

makes 2 fillets

Reel in reluctant fish eaters with tender fish cooked with sweet fruit. Steamed in a foil packet, this family-friendly dish is quick to prepare and a cinch to clean up. For confirmed fish lovers, swap richly flavored salmon in place of the halibut. In place of the mango, try papaya or peach. Serve with an instant brown rice bowl.

1 cup (6 oz/185 g) frozen mango chunks, thawed

2 halibut fillets, each about $1/3$ lb (155 g) and $1^1/4$ in (3 cm) thick

olive oil, as needed

salt and pepper

1 yellow or red tomato, diced

2 tbsp mango nectar or frozen orange juice concentrate

12 fresh mint leaves, or 2 tsp dried mint (optional)

1 Preheat the broiler and line a rimmed baking sheet with foil. Have ready 2 large rectangles of foil to make packets.

2 If desired, cut the mango chunks into a smaller dice that your baby can handle. (They will soften with cooking.)

3 Place 1 halibut fillet on each foil rectangle. Press it with your fingertips to check for pin bones and pull any out. Rub the fish on all sides with olive oil and sprinkle with salt and pepper. Top each piece with half of the mango chunks and half of the tomato and drizzle each with 1 tbsp mango nectar. Close the foil over the fish, rolling up the edges to seal it into a packet.

4 Place the packets on the foil-lined pan and slip under the broiler, about 4 in (10 cm) below the heat source. Cook until the halibut is opaque throughout, about 12 minutes.

5 While the fish cooks, mince the fresh mint leaves, if using. Carefully unwrap the fish packets (hot steam will escape) and sprinkle with the mint. Let cool slightly, cut fish into small pieces, and serve. The fish can be refrigerated for up to 1 day.

green muffins

45 minutes
(mostly hands-off)

freezer safe

makes 20 to
24 muffins

These zucchini muffins cook at a lower temperature than some muffins, which helps them cook evenly and stay moister. If you like, replace a third of the all-purpose flour with whole-wheat flour. Use any summer squash (a good use for summer garden abundance!) and freeze the muffins for up to 6 months.

3 cups (15 oz/470 g) all-purpose flour

1 tsp baking soda

1 tsp baking powder

1 tsp salt

3 large eggs, at room temperature

1 cup (8 fl oz/ 250 ml) canola oil

1 cup (8 oz/250 g) sugar

¼ cup (2 fl oz/ 60 ml) orange juice

3 tsp vanilla extract

2 cups (10 oz/315 g) shredded zucchini (about 2 medium zucchini), squeezed dry

1 Preheat the oven to 325°F (165°C). Line 2 muffin pans with paper liners.

2 In a large bowl, sift or whisk together the flour, baking soda, baking powder, and salt; set aside. In another bowl, whisk the eggs. Add the oil, sugar, orange juice, and vanilla and stir with a whisk or rubber spatula until well combined. Stir in the dry ingredients until just combined. Fold in the shredded zucchini.

3 Spoon the batter into the prepared muffin pans, filling each cup two-thirds full. Remove the liners from any empty cupcake cups and fill halfway with water.

4 Bake until a toothpick inserted in the center of a muffin comes out clean, about 25 minutes. Let cool in the pans for 20 minutes, then transfer the muffins to wire racks. Let cool further or completely, check the temperature, and serve. The muffins can be frozen for up to 6 months in a zippered plastic bag.

loafing around

You can also make this recipe in two 8-by-4-in (20-by-10-cm) loaf pans. Bake for about 40 minutes.

rice pudding with fresh fruit

This very simple rice pudding does not require any baking. A classic nursery treat, the pudding can be enjoyed either warm or cold. This eggless version cooks up less firm than a custard-based rice pudding. As with risotto, using Arborio rice lends a little more creaminess than plain white rice.

½ tbsp unsalted butter

pinch of salt

½ cup (3½ oz/ 105 g) Arborio rice

2 cups (16 fl oz/ 500 ml) whole milk

¼ cup (2 oz/60 g) sugar

1 tsp almond or vanilla extract

½ tsp allspice

1 pint (8 oz/250 g) strawberries, plums, or other fruit, diced

1 In a saucepan over medium-high heat, combine 1 cup (8 fl oz/250 ml) water with the butter and salt. Bring to a boil and add the rice. Return to a boil, stir, and reduce the heat to low. Cook until the rice has absorbed the water but is not quite tender, about 15 minutes.

2 In another saucepan over medium heat, bring the milk, sugar, almond extract, and allspice to a simmer. Add the cooked rice and return to a simmer. Reduce the heat to medium-low and cook until the rice absorbs most of the milk and the mixture becomes silky and thick, 10 to 15 minutes.

3 Spoon the pudding into four small serving dishes. Serve warm, or let cool to room temperature and refrigerate until cool and set. Top with the fruit and serve.

4 To store, cover and refrigerate for up to 3 days.

mini yogurt cupcakes

40 minutes

freezer safe

makes about
40 mini cupcakes

Using yogurt in cupcakes and cakes makes for an especially tender and fluffy crumb. The sweet tanginess of these cupcakes is echoed by a tangy chocolate–sour cream frosting. It's a yummy change from the typical birthday party fare that grown-ups can enjoy as much as the kids.

YOGURT CUPCAKES

2 cups (8 oz/250 g) cake flour

1½ tsp baking powder

¼ tsp salt

2 large eggs, at room temperature

¾ cup (6 oz/185 g) sugar

1 cup (8 oz/250 g) plain whole-milk yogurt

½ tsp vanilla extract

¼ cup (2 oz/60 g) unsalted butter, melted and cooled

FROSTING

1½ cups (9 oz/ 280 g) semisweet chocolate chips

2 cups (16 oz/ 500 g) sour cream, at room temperature

1 Preheat the oven to 350°F (180°C). Line two 24-cup mini cupcake pans with paper liners.

2 Sift the flour, baking powder, and salt together into a bowl; set aside. In another bowl, whisk together the eggs and sugar until combined. Whisk in the yogurt and vanilla, then the cooled melted butter. Whisk in the dry ingredients.

3 Spoon the batter into the prepared cupcake pans, being careful to fill each cup only halfway to two-thirds full. Remove the liners from any empty cupcake cups and fill halfway with water.

4 Bake until the cupcakes are golden and a toothpick inserted in the centers comes out clean, 20 to 25 minutes. Let cool in the pans for 10 minutes, then transfer to wire racks and let cool completely.

5 To make the frosting, put the chocolate chips in a microwave-safe bowl and heat in the microwave in 30-second increments until nearly melted. Stir between heatings. When the chocolate is smooth, let cool to room temperature, then fold in the sour cream.

6 Spread frosting on the top of each cooled cupcake and serve. Unfrosted cupcakes can be stored in the refrigerator for up to 5 days or frozen for up to 6 months in a zippered plastic bag. The frosting can be refrigerated for up to 3 days; warm in the microwave for 1 to 2 minutes before using.

fruit granita

20 minutes
plus freezing time

freezer safe

makes 4 cups
(32 oz/1 kg)

This summertime treat is the Italian forebear of the snow cone. It doesn't require any special equipment and can be made with any kind of juice—or any liquid, in fact. Try making it with coffee for the grown-ups (serve with whipped cream, if you like) or even with red wine (stir in a little citrus juice for sangria flavor!).

½ cup (4 oz/125 g) sugar

3 cups (24 fl oz/ 750 ml) lemonade or orange, grape, cranberry, or other fruit juice

1 In a saucepan over medium-high heat, combine 1 cup (8 fl oz/ 250 ml) water and the sugar. Bring to a boil, stirring to dissolve the sugar. Remove from the heat and let cool to room temperature.

2 Stir the lemonade into the cooled sugar syrup. Pour the mixture into a 13-by-9-in (33-by-23-cm) baking pan or 2 smaller pans. (The granita mixture should be no more than 1 in/2.5 cm deep in the pan.) Freeze for 40 minutes, and then check to see if ice crystals have formed along the edges and the bottom. When crystals have formed, stir and scrape the mixture with a fork to break up the crystals. Return the pan to the freezer.

3 Check the pan 3 or 4 more times, every 40 minutes, stirring and scraping to break up ice crystals each time you check, until no liquid remains. If you forget about the mixture and it freezes solid, don't worry: Let the pan stand at room temperature just until the mixture softens, then run a spoon across the top to shave off pieces of ice. Keep scraping until the whole mixture is like packed snow, then refreeze. Once the mixture is evenly frozen, cover and freeze until ready to serve or up to 3 months.

4 To serve, spoon into small dessert bowls or paper cups.

cool tip

Granita is a good treat to make on the weekend because, although it requires little effort, it does require a few rounds of stirring as it freezes.

birthday cake

45 minutes

freezer safe

makes one 7-in
(18-cm) layer cake

The perfect choice for celebrating your baby's first birthday, this delicious little carrot cake is not too sweet, and it is adorable. Make it in two 7-in (18-cm) cake pans, in 2 mini cupcake pans with 24 cups per pan, or in a rimmed sheet pan, using 4- or 5-in (10- or 13-cm) cutters to make the cake layers.

YOGURT FROSTING

one 32-oz (1-kg) carton vanilla whole-milk yogurt

CARROT CAKE

2 large carrots

1/2 cup (4 fl oz/ 125 ml) canola oil

1/2 cup (3 1/2 oz/ 105 g) firmly packed brown sugar

2 large eggs

1 1/2 cups (7 1/2 oz/ 235 g) all-purpose flour

1 tsp baking soda

1 tsp baking powder

1 tsp ground allspice

1/4 tsp ground nutmeg

1/4 tsp salt

1 To make the frosting, line a large sieve with cheesecloth and set it over a bowl. Pour the yogurt into the sieve and let drain until thickened while you make the cake.

2 Preheat the oven to 400°F (200°C). Spray two 7-in (18-cm) round cake pans with oil and line each with a circle of parchment paper. Using the large holes on a box grater, shred the carrots; you should have about 1 1/2 cups (7 1/2 oz/235 g).

3 In a large bowl, stir together the oil and sugar with a wooden spoon. Stir in the eggs, one at a time. Add the flour, baking soda, baking powder, allspice, nutmeg, and salt and stir until combined. Fold in the grated carrots. The batter will be dense and stiff.

4 Divide the batter evenly between the prepared pans. Bake until a toothpick inserted in the center comes out clean, about 20 minutes. Let the cakes cool in the pans on a wire rack for 10 minutes. Invert onto the racks, peel off the parchment, and let cool completely.

5 Place one cake layer, flat side up, on a serving plate. Use a flexible metal spatula to dollop slightly less than half of the frosting on top and gently smooth and spread just to the edges. Place the other cake layer on top, flat side down, and frost the top in the same way. Cut into wedges and serve. To store, wrap tightly in plastic and refrigerate for up to 5 days or freeze for up to 6 months.

the 5 nutrients babies need

This chart offers a quick overview of the nutrients your baby needs most, and which foods readily provide them. The best way to ensure that your baby gets all the necessary vitamins, minerals, and trace elements is to offer a variety of foods. In the early months, breast milk contains all the essential nutrients, as does commercial formula, provided baby is drinking the recommended amount.

1 Iron

why babies need it

Iron is critical for brain development. Research shows a lack of this mineral can lead to thought-processing and motor deficiencies. The good news is that infants are born with large iron stores, usually enough to satisfy their needs until 4 to 6 months of age. After that, they need to get iron from their food or formula.

daily dose

Formula meets iron needs for the first year, but breast milk doesn't, which is why pediatricians recommend introducing high-iron food early on in the second half of the first year, when you start your baby on solid foods. At 7 to 12 months, babies need 11 milligrams of elemental iron per day, and by 1 to 3 years old, 7 milligrams daily.

serve it up

After your baby is 6 months old, two servings of iron-fortified baby cereal (one-half ounce each) provide the 11 milligrams your baby needs. Meat, poultry, and fish are naturally iron-packed; try giving ground beef or turkey, chicken, and halibut to your little eater. Other rich sources include avocado, potato, beans, broccoli, chickpeas, eggs, and prunes.

good to know

Iron deficiency is the most common nutritional deficiency among U.S. children. To prevent it, make sure your pediatrician screens your baby for iron-deficiency anemia at 12 months and again at 18 months.

2 · Zinc

why babies need it

Besides having a positive effect on cognition and development, zinc's primary roles are to maintain immune function and assure optimal cell growth and repair.

daily dose

Formula meets needs through age 1, but breast milk doesn't, so it's important to introduce zinc-rich foods in the second half of the first year. Children from 7 months to 3 years of age need 3 milligrams a day.

serve it up

Three ounces of pork tenderloin has 2 milligrams, a cup of yogurt has 1.6 milligrams, and half a chicken breast has 1 milligram.

good to know

Zinc is most commonly found in iron-rich meat, poultry and fish, so if you're meeting your baby's iron needs, chances are she's getting enough zinc, too.

3 · Calcium

why babies need it

This mineral helps children achieve peak bone mass, which is necessary for building strong bones and preventing fractures when kids start climbing trees and playing sports.

daily dose

Breast milk and formula meet your baby's calcium needs for the first year. Once you switch to whole milk, your baby will need 500 milligrams daily.

serve it up

A cup of whole milk or 6 ounces of yogurt each provides about 250 milligrams. Babies under age 1 shouldn't have cow's milk, but yogurt is typically fine once you have introduced solids (see page 38).

good to know

Babies who are at risk for obesity or who have a strong family history of early-onset cardiovascular disease can have 2 percent milk between 12 and 24 months.

4

Vitamins A, D, E, and K

why babies need it

Vitamin A promotes proper vision and healthy skin. Vitamin D increases calcium absorption and helps with bone growth—a deficiency can cause bone-weakening rickets. Vitamin E's antioxidant powers facilitate cell growth and the development of the nervous system. Vitamin K helps with normal blood clotting.

daily dose

Infant formula meets needs through age 1 for vitamins A, D, and E. To get enough vitamin D, breastfed babies should take a supplement that provides 400 IU of vitamin D daily until they are weaned from the breast or are taking 15 or more ounces of formula daily. Otherwise, if you offer your baby a variety of foods—fruits, vegetables, dairy, whole grains, healthy fats—and your doctor says she is growing appropriately for her age, she is likely meeting her needs for these vitamins.

serve it up

Beyond breast milk, formula, and cow's milk, good sources of vitamin A include carotene-rich fruits and vegetables such as carrots, sweet potatoes, and broccoli. Vitamin D occurs in few foods—which is why the AAP recommends a daily supplement for breastfed babies—but your baby can get some from fortified cow's milk, egg yolks, and fish. Vitamin E-rich foods include vegetable oils, cereals, and grains. Cow's milk, leafy vegetables, fruit, and soybean oil are full of vitamin K.

good to know

A recent study found that 40 percent of infants and toddlers have low levels of vitamin D, which can weaken bones. Make sure you talk to your pediatrician about starting your baby on a vitamin D supplement if you are breastfeeding.

5

Vitamins B and C

why babies need it

Vitamin C improves iron absorption and helps prevent scurvy, a condition that causes large bruises on the body. B-complex vitamins, including folic acid, enhance the immune and nervous systems, maintain healthy skin and muscle tone, promote cell growth, and regulate metabolism.

daily dose

If you offer your baby a variety of foods from the food pyramid—fruits, vegetables, dairy, whole grains, healthy fats—and your doctor says she is growing appropriately for her age, she is likely getting enough of these water-soluble vitamins (meaning they are not stored in the body and must be replaced daily).

serve it up

Vitamin C is in citrus, tomatoes, strawberries, melon, and potatoes. Folic acid is in green vegetables and fortified cereals and breads. The other B vitamins are found in whole grains like brown rice as well as in bananas, beans, eggs, meat, poultry, and fish.

good to know

Don't give up on the green stuff or other nutrient-rich fruits and vegetables! Most toddlers have to try a food—as in, literally put it in their mouths and spit it out—an average of eight to 10 times (or more!) before they start to accept it.

index

Copyright © 2010 Weldon Owen Inc.

Library of Congress Cataloging-in-Publication
data is available.

ISBN: 978-0-8118-7131-0
Manufactured in China

Design by Ashley Lima
Food styling by Kevin Crafts

Additional photography courtesy of Digital Vision/GettyImages:
page 1 (middle), page 106; Corbis/Jupiterimages: page 7;
Andrew Olney/Photodisc/GettyImages: page 9; Emma Boys:
page 12; Lauren Burke/Photodisc/GettyImages: page 34;
Absodels/GettyImages: page 62.

Conceived and produced by Weldon Owen Inc.
415 Jackson Street, Suite 200, San Francisco, CA 94111
Telephone: 415 291 0100 Fax: 415 291 8841

Weldon Owen wishes to thank the following people for their
support in producing this book: Lisa Atwood, Natalie Hoelen,
Elizabeth Parson, Ann Sackrider, David Sackrider, Kate Washington,
Sharron Wood, and Jack Campion Wright.

10 9 8 7 6 5 4 3 2 1

Chronicle Books LLC
680 Second Street
San Francisco, CA 94107

www.chroniclebooks.com